LET'S EAT

Indian

LET'S EAT
Indian

Gupta-Lal-Singh

Editor
Wendy Hobson

foulsham
LONDON • NEW YORK • TORONTO • SYDNEY

foulsham

Bennetts Close, Cippenham, Berkshire SL1 5AP

ISBN 0-572-01728-6

Copyright © 1992 Strathearn Publishing Ltd.

Photoset in Great Britain by Typesetting Solutions, Slough, Berks.
Printed in Great Britain by Cox & Wyman Ltd, Reading, Berks.

Contents

Introduction

If you enjoy eating out in Indian restaurants and want to try preparing your favourite meals at home, then this book is for you. Simple step-by-step instructions show you how to create well-known dishes such as Tandoori Chicken, Rogan Josh, Chicken Korma and Onion Bhajis in your own kitchen. A typical Indian meal often starts with drinks — perhaps a refreshing sherbet — and some savoury snacks. Then, when everyone is seated at the table, there will be a starter, followed by one or two meat dishes, a vegetable curry or dhal, a rice dish and a bread — paratha, chappati or naan — with which to scoop up the food. There will also be a selection of accompaniments such as raita, popadums, relishes and chutneys. Drinks are usually non-alcoholic, because spicy food doesn't go very well with wine. *Lassi* (yoghurt and water) or iced water with a slice of lemon are often served. The dessert may be fresh fruit or the Indian ice cream, *kulfi.* Coffee or tea are drunk after the meal, and sometimes aniseeds or small cardamom seeds in their husks are offered as an aid to digestion.

Each region of India has its own distinctive style of cooking. Tandoor and moghlai dishes originate in the northern states of Punjab, Kashmir, Uttar Pradesh and Delhi. Variations in soil and climate influence regional products and this is reflected in the cuisine. Coconuts, tamarind and curry leaves are plentiful in the south and are used in the dishes from that region. Madras curries are flavoured with coconut, for example.

Preparing Indian food is not as difficult as you might think. It depends heavily on herbs and spices for those wonderful flavours, and these are now easy to find in most large supermarkets. To start with, it's a good idea to buy only those you need for a specific dish and then gradually increase your store cupboard as you increase your expertise. Whole spices will keep for a long time in airtight jars.

Meat and poultry are often marinated for several hours in a mixture of yoghurt and spices before cooking. This tenderises the meat and enables the flavour of the spices to penetrate thoroughly — the longer you leave the food to marinate, the better it tastes.

Ingredients

Many of the ingredients used in Indian cooking can be readily found in supermarkets. For the more unusual ones you may have to look in delicatessens, health food shops or Asian food stores.

Coconut

Madras curries from southern India are flavoured with coconut and it is also used in other dishes. Prepared desiccated coconut is the easiest to use, but you will get the best flavour from fresh grated coconut. If you buy and grate a whole coconut you can freeze it in small batches to use later. Some recipes use coconut oil, which is available in supermarkets and delicatessens.

Dhals

Many types of dhal, or pulses, are used in Indian cooking. The best known ones, chick peas and lentils, are available in supermarkets and the more unusual varieties can be bought in health food shops or Asian stores. Dried pulses will keep for up to a year if stored in an airtight container. Packets of dhals often contain small stones and husks, so they need to be picked over and washed in several changes of water before use. Whole pulses should be soaked overnight in cold water before cooking.

Besan, or gram flour, is made from ground chick peas. This fine yellow flour is high in protein but low in gluten. It is available in Asian food shops. *Sev* is a snack made from gram flour.

Fruit

Fresh fruit is often served at the end of an Indian meal: mangoes, pineapples, guavas, melon, bananas, or whatever is in season. Lime juice is a common ingredient in many recipes and the juice from ripe tamarind pods is used to give a sharp taste. If you cannot find this in Asian food shops, you can substitute lemon juice, although this does not give quite the same distinctive taste.

Garam Masala

This strong and aromatic blend of spices is often sprinkled on a finished dish. It is best to make your own garam masala rather than use a commercial brand, although it is readily available in supermarkets. It is best to roast the spices in a wok, on a griddle or in the oven before grinding them.

To make about 90 ml/6 tbsp of garam masala, roast and then grind the following ingredients to a fine powder: 2-3 x 5 cm/2 in cinnamon sticks, 10 cloves, 8 ml/1 heaped tsp of whole black peppercorns, seeds of 5 black cardamoms, 5-6 whole green cardamoms, 5 ml/1 tsp freshly grated nutmeg (optional).

Ghee

Indian food is often cooked in ghee, or clarified butter, because it can be heated to a high temperature without burning. Ghee can be bought in Asian food shops or you can prepare it yourself using unsalted butter. Melt the butter in a saucepan and simmer it gently for about 20 minutes until it becomes clear and a whitish residue settles at the bottom. Remove from the heat, spoon off any scum on the surface and allow to cool. The clear liquid can then be strained off into a container and will keep for 3 or 4 months in the refrigerator.

Herbs and Spices

Indian food contains many varied herbs and spices which add flavour and colour. Most of these are available in a supermarket. For the best flavour, buy spices in their whole form and grind them as you need them — either in a food processor or with a pestle and mortar. The spices will keep well in an airtight jar. Dry roasting spices in a frying pan produces a wonderful aroma and increases their flavour.

Aniseed: These liquorice-flavoured seeds are widely used in the preparation of confectionery, liqueurs and sweet chutneys. They also give an unusual flavour to meat dishes, such as Bhuna Ghosht.

Asafoetida: The horrible smell of this spice disappears in the cooking process. It is used in very small quantities to flavour meat, fish and vegetable dishes, and also aids digestion. Asafoetida is the milky sap of a giant fennel plant and it solidifies into a pale rust-brown resin. You can buy it in powdered form in Asian food shops. Store it in an airtight tin.

Cardamom: There are two varieties of cardamom — large black ones and small green ones — and they can be used whole (in which case you leave them on the side of your plate as they are not meant to be eaten) or ground.

Chilli: Fresh green chillies are used in many Indian recipes and you should vary the amount you use to suit your own taste. If you chop them by hand, make sure you wash your hands thoroughly afterwards, and also wash the knife and chopping board, because chillies contain an irritant that causes painful stinging if you touch your mouth or eyes. Red chillies are smaller and these are often fried for a few seconds until they puff up and the skin darkens. The fried skin adds a special flavour to a dish. You can use the seeds if you like dishes very hot, or discard them and just use the flesh. Red and green chillies are also available dried.

Chilli powder is available in varying degrees of hotness. Use it sparingly otherwise it will mask other flavours, and vary the quantities to suit your own taste.

Cinnamon: This is the dried, rolled bark of a tropical evergreen tree, and you buy it in small sticks or in a powdered form. The sticks are used to flavour meat and vegetable dishes and are not meant to be eaten.

Cloves: These are the dried flower buds of an Asiatic tree and can be used whole (when they are not meant to be eaten) or ground. They are used as a flavouring in many curries.

Coriander: Fresh green coriander is often used as a garnish, rather as parsley is used in British dishes. The small beige-coloured seeds are sometimes used whole but more usually ground.

Cumin: These caraway-like seeds are used frequently in Indian cooking, either whole or ground. To roast cumin seeds, heat a heavy-based frying pan and dry roast the seeds for a few minutes until beginning to brown. Then crush them with a mortar and pestle.

Curry leaves: Usually sold dried, these are the leaves of a tree that grows in India. They are used for flavouring and should be removed before serving.

Fenugreek: Small, dark orange-coloured fenugreek seeds are used in curry powder and give it the characteristic smell. Ground fenugreek is also used. The seeds can be sprouted to provide a leafy vegetable that is sometimes cooked like spinach.

Garam masala: see above.

Ginger: Fresh root ginger is an essential ingredient in many Indian dishes. It needs to be peeled before grating or chopping. Dried and powdered ginger is not a good substitute.

Nutmeg: It is best to buy whole nutmegs and grate them yourself because the flavour of this spice is quickly lost. Nutmeg has a warm, sweet, nutty flavour and is used in both sweet and savoury dishes.

Onion seeds: These small black seeds are collected from shoots produced by the onion plant. They are used in both sweet and savoury dishes, and sometimes sprinkled on to naan bread before it is baked.

Paprika: This ground red powder is used to add colour to a dish. It has a much milder flavour than cayenne or chilli powder.

Peppercorns: Black ones are used in savoury snacks and biryanis and the powdered form in raitas and pickles. The peppercorns should always be freshly ground as they quickly lose their flavour.

Poppy seeds: These are used to add a nutty flavour to many dishes.

Saffron: Saffron fronds are the stigmas of crocuses that grow in the northern state of Kashmir. Saffron is used to colour and flavour pilau, biryani, sweets, puddings and cakes. A solution of saffron can be made by crushing the fronds and then steeping them in hot water or milk for 10 minutes. Powdered saffron is sold in some supermarkets, although this is even more expensive than saffron strands. Turmeric is often substituted for saffron, but this does not have the same exquisite flavour.

Sesame seeds: Added to naan bread, sesame seeds give a wonderful nutty flavour. They are rich in protein and oil.

Tandoori spices: see below.

Turmeric: This bright yellow powder is used to colour a dish as well as impart its distinctive flavour.

Tandoori Spices

The traditional tandoori spices impart a wonderful colour as well as flavour to chicken or meat. You can make your own tandoori marinade. This quantity is sufficient to coat about 900 g/2 lb of chicken or meat. Ideally, the meat should be left to marinate overnight, but if you are in a hurry a minimum of two hours would do. You can omit the food colouring if you prefer.

Mix together: 45 ml/3 tbsp lightly beaten natural yoghurt, juice of 3 small limes, 45 ml/3 tbsp ground garlic, 15 ml/1 tbsp ground ginger, red chilli powder to taste, 5 ml/1 tsp ground coriander, salt to taste, a few drops of red food colouring (optional). Make a few gashes in the chicken or meat and rub the mixed ingredients well into the pieces of meat.

Vegetables

Many Indians are vegetarians, so there is a wide variety of vegetable dishes in Indian cuisine. Those used in the recipes in this book — potatoes, aubergines, cauliflower, okra, carrots, broccoli, spinach, mushrooms and peas — can all be bought in a supermarket or greengrocer. When you are using several different vegetables in the same recipe they should all be cut to the same size. This not only creates a good impression, it ensures even cooking.

Vindaloo Powder

You can buy a vindaloo powder from Indian food shops, or you can make your own.

Roast a small piece of cinnamon stick, 5 ml/1 tsp cloves, 10 ml/2 tsp cumin seeds, 45 ml/3 tbsp coriander seeds, 10 ml/2 tsp mustard seeds, 5 ml/1 tsp black peppercorns and 6 red chillies in a dry frying pan or on a griddle. The spices should brown lightly and become aromatic. Grind them finely and add 10 ml/2 tsp turmeric. Mix well and store in an airtight jar.

Yoghurt

Yoghurt, or *dahi*, is widely used in Indian cooking and in *raita* is served as an accompaniment to spicy dishes. A recipe for making your own yoghurt is given on page 142.

Equipment

You don't need special utensils or equipment for cooking Indian food — what you already have in the kitchen will be perfectly suitable.

Food Processor

You will need a food processor or pestle and mortar for grinding your spices.

Pressure Cooker

While not essential, you can cook many Indian dishes in a pressure cooker, which will substantially reduce the cooking times.

Saucepans

Heavy-based frying pans and saucepans are recommended because they spread the heat more evenly and are better for the long, slow cooking that is usually required for Indian dishes.

Skewers

Indian kebabs require skewers, *seekh,* on which to thread the ingredients. Metal or wooden skewers are perfect. Wooden skewers should be soaked in water before using to prevent them charring while the food is cooking.

Indian Equipment

If you want to splash out and buy some Indian equipment, then a *tawa,* or iron griddle is a useful item for making breads and dry roasting seeds. A *kerai,* a semi-spherical aluminium or iron pan, saves a lot of oil if you are frying food. In some parts of India a *tandoor,* a clay oven, is used to cook food at a very high temperature, but an ordinary oven is perfectly adequate for making delicious tandoori dishes. A *balti* is a pan like a wok.

Notes on the Recipes

1. Follow one set of measurements only, do not mix metric and Imperial.

2. Eggs are size 2.

3. Wash fresh produce before preparation.

4. Spoon measurements are level.

5. Adjust seasoning and strongly flavoured ingredients, such as onions and garlic, to suit your own taste.

6. If you substitute dried for fresh herbs, use only half the amount specified.

Appetisers

Snacks are very popular in India. They may be served as starters to a meal, or as light dishes for afternoon tea. Often a sherbet, lassi, is offered as a drink to accompany them. In Indian cities there are kebab and samosa stalls on every corner, and they are consumed in the street as we in the West eat hot dogs and hamburgers. These recipes include many dishes that you will find on Indian restaurant menus as appetisers for a main meal.

1 | Tandoori King Prawns

Ingredients

30 ml/2 tbsp lemon juice
10 ml/2 tsp ground ginger
2 green chillies, seeded and chopped
Salt and freshly ground black pepper
450 g/1 lb shelled king prawns
30 ml/2 tbsp natural yoghurt, lightly beaten
2.5 ml/½ tsp garam masala
50 g/2 oz butter or ghee, melted
1 lemon, finely sliced

Method

1. Grind together the lemon juice, ginger, chillies, salt and pepper.

2. Rub the mixture into the prawns and leave to stand for 10 minutes.

3. Mix together the yoghurt and garam masala. Pour over the prawns and stir to coat well. Leave to stand for 30 minutes.

4. Thread the prawns on to skewers and arrange them on a rack in a roasting tin so that the juices can drain off the prawns. Bake in a preheated oven at 160°C/325°F/gas mark 3 for 5 minutes.

5. Brush with the butter or ghee and return to the oven for a further 5 minutes until crisp. Serve garnished with the lemon slices.

Serves 4

2 Tandoori Chicken

Ingredients

4 cm/1 ½ in piece ginger root
1 clove garlic
2 onions, sliced into rings
300 ml/½ pt/1 ¼ cups natural yoghurt
1 medium chicken, skinned and cut into serving pieces
2 cinnamon sticks
1 bay leaf
10 cloves
8 black peppercorns
3 cardamoms, peeled and crushed
150 ml/¼ pt/⅔ cup lemon juice
10 ml/2 tsp chilli powder
5 ml/1 tsp cumin seeds
Salt
50 g/2 oz butter or ghee, melted
5 ml/1 tsp garam masala
1 lemon, sliced

Method

1. Grind together the ginger, garlic, 1 onion and the yoghurt.

2. Spread the mixture all over the chicken pieces and leave to marinate for 5 hours.

3. Grind together the cinnamon, bay leaf, cloves, peppercorns and cardamoms. Mix with the lemon juice, chilli powder and cumin seeds. Make slashes with a sharp knife on the chicken pieces and smear them with the mixture. Sprinkle with salt and leave to stand for 1 hour.

4. Thread the chicken pieces on to skewers, brush them with melted butter or ghee and grill on a

barbecue, if possible, or under a grill, turning frequently, for about 30 minutes until cooked through. Alternatively roast in a preheated oven at 200°C/400°F/gas mark 6.

5. Sprinkle with garam masala and serve garnished with the lemon slices and remaining onion rings.

Serves 6 to 8

3 Tandoori Fish

Ingredients

4 cm/1 ½ in piece ginger root
8 cloves garlic
5 cm/2 in cube green papaya (optional)
5 ml/1 tsp turmeric
2.5 ml/½ tsp cumin seeds
15 ml/1 tbsp chilli powder
Juice of 2 lemons
Salt
1 x 900 g/2 lb white fish, gutted and scaled
45 ml/3 tbsp vegetable oil
15 ml/1 tbsp garam masala
1 lemon, sliced

Method

1. Grind the ginger, garlic, papaya, if using, turmeric, cumin seeds, chilli powder, lemon juice and salt to a smooth paste. Rub the paste all over the fish, inside and outside including the head. Make 4 gashes on either side of the fish with a sharp knife. Leave to stand in a cool place for 1 hour.

2. Pierce the fish lengthways on a long skewer. Heat the oil and brush the fish with the oil. Grill, turning occasionally, for about 20 minutes until the fish is lightly browned, brushing frequently with the oil. Alternatively, bake in a preheated oven at 200°C/400°F/gas mark 6.

3. When the fish is barely cooked, sprinkle with garam masala and continue to cook until dark golden brown. Serve garnished with lemon slices.

Serves 4 to 6

4 Chicken Tikka

Ingredients

5 ml/1 tsp ground ginger
2 cloves garlic, crushed
5 ml/1 tsp ground white pepper
Salt
12 chicken breasts, cut into chunks
1 egg, lightly beaten
50 g/2 oz Cheddar cheese, grated
2 green chillies, seeded and chopped
30 ml/2 tbsp finely chopped fresh coriander
150 ml/¼ pt/⅔ cup cream, lightly beaten
2.5 ml/½ tsp grated nutmeg
2.5 ml/½ tsp ground mace
45 ml/3 tbsp cornflour
Butter or vegetable oil for basting

Method

1. Mix together the ginger, garlic, pepper and salt and rub into the chicken pieces. Leave to stand for 15 minutes.

2. Whisk together all the remaining ingredients except the butter or oil. Pour over the chicken and leave to marinate in a cool place for at least 5 hours, or overnight if possible.

3. Thread the chicken pieces on to skewers and arrange on a rack in a baking tin lined with kitchen foil so that the juices can drain off the skewers. Cook in a preheated oven at 180°C/ 350°F/gas mark 4 for about 15 minutes, basting occasionally with the butter or oil, until cooked through and crisp.

Serves 6

5 | Lamb Tikka

These flavoursome pieces of meat make excellent starters and can also be served as cocktail snacks.

Ingredients

5 ml/1 tsp ground ginger
1 clove garlic, crushed
2.5 ml/½ tsp ground cinnamon
2.5 ml/½ tsp chilli powder
Salt
450 g/1 lb boned lamb, cubed
30 ml/2 tbsp natural yoghurt
5 ml/1 tsp ground fenugreek
5 ml/1 tsp ground coriander
Butter or vegetable oil for basting

Method

1.   Mix together the ginger, garlic, cinnamon, chilli powder and salt. Rub the mixture well into the meat.

2.   Mix together all the remaining ingredients except the butter or oil and pour over the meat. Stir to coat it well. Leave to marinate in the refrigerator for at least 5 hours.

3.   Drain the pieces of meat and thread them on to skewers, leaving a little gap between each piece. Arrange the skewers on a rack in a baking tin lined with kitchen foil so that the juices drain off the skewers. Cook in a preheated oven at 180°C/350°F/gas mark 4 for about 15 minutes until cooked through and crisp.

Serves 6

6 Seekh Kebabs

Ingredients

1 onion, chopped into thick pieces
15 ml/1 tbsp chopped ginger root
10 ml/2 tsp ground cinnamon
2.5 ml/½ tsp chilli powder
450 g/1 lb minced beef
5 ml/1 tsp ground mango (amchoor) or 10 ml/2 tsp
   lemon juice
30 ml/2 tbsp natural yoghurt
30 ml/2 tbsp gram flour
30 ml/2 tbsp finely chopped fresh coriander
5 ml/1 tsp salt

Method

1. Purée the onion, ginger, cinnamon and chilli powder to a paste.

2. Mix the purée with the meat, ground mango or lemon juice, yoghurt, gram flour, coriander and salt and knead well.

3. Turn the mixture on to a floured surface and roll it like a smooth dough. Take small portions of the mixture and wrap it round skewers to make sausage shapes.

4. Grill the kebabs under a hot grill for about 20 minutes, turning frequently, until cooked through and crisp.

Serves 4

7 | Samosas

These little pastries stuffed with a spicy filling are very popular as a snack with drinks, or as a starter to a meal.

Ingredients

150 g/5 oz/1 ¼ cups plain flour
5 ml/1 tsp salt
2.5 ml/½ tsp baking powder
25 g/1 oz butter or ghee
90 ml/6 tbsp water
225 g/8 oz minced meat
2.5 ml/½ tsp turmeric
30 ml/2 tbsp vegetable oil
1 onion, thinly sliced
2.5 ml/½ tsp chilli powder
5 ml/1 tsp sugar
5 ml/1 tsp cumin seeds, roasted and ground
Vegetable oil for deep-frying

Method

1. Sift the flour, 2.5 ml/½ tsp of salt and the baking powder into a bowl. Rub in the butter or ghee. Mix in about 30 ml/2 tbsp of water to make a soft smooth dough. Cover with a damp tea towel and leave on one side.

2. Place the meat, turmeric, remaining 2.5 ml/½ tsp salt and 60 ml/4 tbsp of water in a saucepan and brown the meat, stirring continuously. Cook over a low heat for about 15 minutes until the meat is cooked. Drain off the liquid.

3. Heat the oil in a separate pan and fry the onion until lightly browned. Add the meat, chilli powder

and sugar and cook for 5 minutes. Add the cumin and cook for a further 2 minutes. Leave to cool.

4. Knead the prepared dough and divide it into 8 portions. Shape each one into a ball then roll it out on a floured surface until as thin as possible. Cut each piece in half.

5. Take a semi-circle of dough in your hands, brush the edges of the cut side with a little water and press them together to seal. Put some of the meat mixture inside this cone, brush the remaining edges with water and seal them together. Prepare the remaining samosas in the same way.

6. Heat the oil and fry the samosas a few at a time for about 8 minutes until golden brown. Drain well on kitchen paper and serve hot or cold.

7. As a variation, you can use vegetables instead of meat for the filling. Try potatoes, boiled and cubed; or a mixture of potatoes, peas, diced carrots and cauliflower. Add 5 ml/1 tsp of garam masala to the spices.

Makes 16 samosas

8 Stuffed Parathas

Use one of the stuffings to this quantity of dough.

Ingredients

150 g/5 oz/1 ¼ cups plain flour
2.5 ml/½ tsp salt
2.5 ml/½ tsp baking powder
25 g/1 oz butter or ghee
30 ml/2 tbsp water

For potato stuffing:
225 g/8 oz cooked mashed potato
1 onion, minced and fried
15 ml/1 tbsp chopped fresh parsley
2.5 ml/½ tsp salt
2.5 ml/½ tsp aniseed
A pinch of ground ginger
A pinch of paprika
5 ml/1 tsp lime juice

For cauliflower stuffing:
150 g/6 oz cauliflower, chopped and sautéed in butter
15 ml/1 tbsp grated ginger root
15 ml/1 tbsp ground pomegranate seeds
5 ml/1 tsp ground cumin
2.5 ml/½ tsp salt

30 ml/2 tbsp plain flour
25 g/1 oz ghee

Method

1. Sift the flour, salt and baking powder into a bowl. Rub in the butter or ghee. Mix in enough water to make a soft smooth dough. Cover with a damp tea towel and leave on one side.

2.   Mix together all the ingredients for your chosen stuffing.

3.   Knead the prepared dough and divide it into 16 portions. Shape each one into a ball then roll it out on a floured surface until as thin as possible.

4.   Put a little stuffing on to the centre of 8 dough circles, brush the edges with water and cover with a second circle of dough. Press down the edges, fold in half and press into a triangular shape. Roll out again on a floured surface to make a large triangle. Repeat with the remaining circles.

5.   Heat a frying pan and cook the parathas for about 30 seconds on each side. Add the ghee to the pan and cook for a further 10 minutes, turning frequently, until the parathas have golden brown spots on both sides. Serve hot.

Makes 8

9 Sag Pakora

Ingredients

225 g/8 oz spinach leaves
225 g/8 oz/2 cups gram flour
45 ml/3 tbsp lemon juice
5 ml/1 tsp chilli powder
5 ml/1 tsp ground ginger
2.5 ml/½ tsp freshly ground black pepper
A pinch of turmeric
250 ml/8 fl oz/1 cup water
Vegetable oil for deep-frying

Method

1. Trim most of the stems from the spinach leaves. Wash and leave to drain thoroughly.

2. Mix together the gram flour, lemon juice, chilli powder, ginger, pepper and turmeric. Gradually add the water, whisking until you have a smooth fairly thin batter.

3. Heat the oil in a deep frying pan or wok until a tiny drop of batter rises to the surface immediately.

4. Dip a spinach leaf in the batter and drop it into the oil. Fry the leaves in batches for a few minutes until golden brown on both sides. Drain on kitchen paper and serve hot.

Serves 4

10 Sag Bhajis

Ingredients

100 g/4 oz/1 cup gram flour
5 ml/1 tsp salt
2.5 ml/1 tsp chilli powder
150 ml/¼ pt/⅔ cup water
2 green chillies, seeded and chopped
15 ml/1 tbsp finely chopped fresh coriander
5 ml/1 tsp melted butter or ghee
Vegetable oil for deep-frying
100 g/4 oz spinach leaves, finely shredded

Method

1. Sift the flour, salt and chilli powder into a bowl and add just enough water to make a thick batter. Beat well until smooth then leave to stand for 30 minutes.

2. Stir the chillies and coriander into the batter then add the melted butter or ghee.

3. Heat the oil in a deep frying pan. Dip small balls of spinach into the batter, drop into the hot oil and deep-fry for about 5 minutes until crisp and golden. Drain on kitchen paper and serve hot.

Serves 4

11 | Onion Bhajis

Ingredients

100 g/4 oz/1 cup gram flour
2 onions, finely chopped
1 green chilli, seeded and chopped
5 ml/1 tsp finely chopped fresh coriander
A pinch of bicarbonate of soda
Salt
150 ml/¼ pt/⅔ cup water
Vegetable oil for frying
250 ml/8 fl oz/1 cup Yoghurt Mint Sauce (page 146)

Method

1. Put all the ingredients except the water, oil and sauce into a bowl and gradually mix in just enough water to make a thick batter. Leave to stand for 30 minutes.

2. Heat 2.5 cm/1 in depth of oil in a wok or heavy-based frying pan almost to smoking point. Turn down the heat to minimum and wait for 5 minutes.

3. Start dropping in the batter in large tablespoonfuls. Fry each batch for about 4 minutes until light brown. Remove from the oil and drain on kitchen paper. You can prepare the bhajis to this stage in advance.

4. When you are ready to eat, break the fried bhajis into small bite-sized pieces. Heat the oil and fry the pieces until golden brown and crisp. Serve with the yoghurt mint sauce.

Serves 4 to 5

12 | Mushroom Bhajis

Ingredients

100 g/4 oz/1 cup gram flour
5 ml/1 tsp salt
2.5 ml/½ tsp chilli powder
150 ml/¼ pt/⅔ cup water
1 green chilli, seeded and finely chopped
15 ml/1 tbsp finely chopped fresh coriander
5 ml/1 tsp melted butter or ghee
Vegetable oil for deep-frying
100 g/4 oz button mushrooms

Method

1. Sift the flour, salt and chilli powder into a bowl and add just enough water to make a thick batter. Beat well until smooth then leave to stand for 30 minutes.

2. Stir the chillies and coriander into the batter then add the melted butter or ghee.

3. Heat the oil in a deep frying pan. Dip the mushrooms into the batter, drop into the hot oil and deep-fry for about 5 minutes until crisp and golden. Drain on kitchen paper and serve hot.

Serves 4

13 | Corn Chat

Ingredients

3 potatoes
45 ml/3 tbsp vegetable oil
A pinch of asafoetida
2 large onions, chopped
2 green chillies, seeded and chopped
5 ml/1 tsp ground cumin
2.5 ml/½ tsp garam masala
Salt
225 g/8 oz sweet corn
Juice of 1 lime
10 ml/2 tsp sugar
250 ml/8 fl oz/1 cup sev
30 ml/2 tbsp chopped fresh coriander

Method

1. Boil the potatoes in their skins, cool completely then peel and cut into cubes.

2. Heat the oil and fry the asafoetida for a few seconds. Add the potatoes and fry for about 10 minutes until light golden. Remove from the pan.

3. Add the onions to the pan, with a little more oil if necessary, and fry for about 10 minutes until lightly browned. Add the chillies, cumin, garam masala and salt and fry for a further 30 seconds. Add the corn and potatoes and mix all the ingredients together well.

4. Mix together the lime juice and sugar until the sugar has dissolved then mix into the pan. Remove from the heat. Check and adjust the seasoning to taste.

5. Arrange the mixture on a warmed serving plate

and sprinkle with the *sev* and coriander. Serve hot or cold with Indian chutney.

6.   As a variation, omit the *sev* and reduce the lime juice if you prefer. The dish can then be served as a vegetable.

Serves 6

 Aloo Chat

Ingredients

900 g/2 lb small potatoes
4 green chillies, seeded and chopped
5 ml/1 tsp ground mango (amchoor)
5 ml/1 tsp garam masala
5 ml/1 tsp cumin seeds, roasted and ground
150 ml/¼ pt/⅔ cup lemon juice
5 ml/1 tsp chopped fresh coriander
Salt

Method

1.   Wash the potatoes thoroughly and boil them in their skins. Peel and slice into small rounds.

2.   Place in a serving bowl and mix in all the remaining ingredients.

Serves 6

15 | Popadums

Round, wafer-thin and flat when uncooked, these popadums — as they are called in the south, they are called papad in the north — are very much taken for granted in most Indian homes. They are made in a variety of ways: from pulses, rice flour, potato or sago; flavoured with pepper, chilli and various spices. You can buy partially-prepared popadums in packets and all you have to do is cook them.

There is a small, round, white popadum that becomes fluffy and light when fried. Other varieties are a brownish colour when you buy them and these can be fried or roasted. These taste different, and are certainly healthier.

Popadums are served as an accompaniment at meals, and are sometimes served with a selection of Indian chutneys and an Onion Salad (page 42) while guests are waiting for a starter. They are also enjoyably addictive with an evening drink.

Ingredients

250 ml/8 fl oz/1 cup vegetable oil
8 ready-prepared popadums

Method

1. To fry popadums, heat the oil in a wok or heavy-based frying pan. Drop in one popadum at a time and fry for a few seconds until the popadum swells up and floats to the surface. Remove and drain on kitchen paper while you fry the remaining popadums. Do not let the popadums get too brown or they will be overcooked and taste slightly bitter.

2. To roast popadums, hold a popadum directly over a flame for a few seconds, turning continuously from one side to the other. When cooked, it will be brown with dark patches over it.

3. Place 1 or 2 popadums at a time on a plate in the microwave and microwave on high for about 40 seconds.

Serves 4

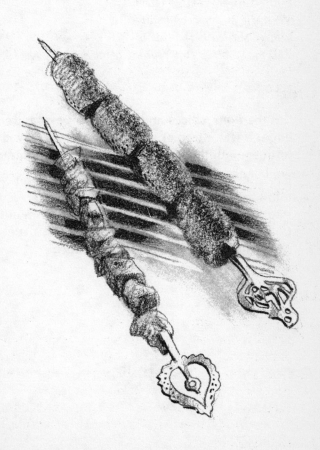

16 King Prawn Butterfly

Ingredients

100 g/4 oz/1 cup gram flour
5 ml/1 tsp garam masala
5 ml/1 tsp paprika
5 ml/1 tsp salt
150 ml/¼ pt/⅔ cup water
Vegetable oil for deep-frying
4 large shelled king prawns
250 ml/¼ pt/⅔ cup Yoghurt Mint Sauce (page 146)

Method

1. Sift the flour, spices and salt into a bowl and just enough water to make a thick batter. Beat well until smooth then leave to stand for 30 minutes.

2. Heat the oil in a deep frying pan. Dip the prawns into the batter so that they are well coated, drop into the hot oil and deep-fry for about 3 minutes until crisp and golden. Drain on kitchen paper and serve hot with the yoghurt mint sauce.

Serves 4

Soups

*Soup is not commonly served in
India, although, mainly due to
the British influence, some
Western soups have been adapted
and given an authentic Indian
flavour.*

Lentil Soup

Ingredients

225 g/8 oz/1 cup yellow lentils
750 ml/1 ¼ pts/3 cups water
2.5 ml/½ tsp turmeric
A pinch of ground cumin
A pinch of chilli powder
A pinch of ground coriander
5 ml/1 tsp salt
5 ml/1 tsp sugar
30 ml/2 tbsp vegetable oil or ghee
2.5 ml/½ tsp cumin seeds
2 bay leaves

Method

1. Heat a heavy-based saucepan and dry roast the lentils over a low heat for 5 minutes, stirring continuously. Wash the lentils in fresh water.

2. Put the lentils back into the pan and add the water. Bring to the boil, cover and simmer for 30 minutes.

3. Add the turmeric, cumin, chilli powder and coriander and simmer for a further 15 minutes or until the lentils are soft.

4. Add the salt and sugar.

5. Heat the oil or ghee in a frying pan and fry the cumin seeds and bay leaves gently for 2 to 3 minutes. Pour over the lentils and serve hot.

Serves 4

2 | Mulligatawny Soup

There are hundreds of recipes for mulligatawny soup in India. It is a hearty soup that can almost be a meal in itself.

Ingredients

30 ml/2 tbsp butter or ghee
2 onions, finely chopped
225 g/8 oz/1 cup red lentils, washed and drained
2 carrots, diced
2 tomatoes, skinned and diced
8 curry leaves
1 litre/1 ¾ pts/4 ½ cups water
Salt
2.5 cm/1 in piece ginger root
6 black peppercorns
5 ml/1 tsp ground coriander
1 green chilli, seeded
2.5 ml/½ tsp turmeric
120 ml/4 fl oz/½ cup coconut milk
½ lemon, sliced

Method

1. Heat the butter or ghee in a heavy-based saucepan and fry the onions gently until soft.

2. Add the lentils, carrots, tomatoes, curry leaves, water and salt and bring to the boil.

3. Grind together the ginger, peppercorns, coriander, chilli and turmeric and add to the pan. Cover and simmer gently for about 30 minutes until everything is soft.

4. Purée or rub through a sieve and return to the pan. Add the coconut milk and simmer gently for a further 5 minutes. Serve garnished with the lemon slices.

Serves 4

3 Split Pea Soup

Ingredients

350 g/12 oz/1 ½ cups split peas, soaked overnight
in 1.2 litres/2 pts/5 cups water
5 ml/1 tsp ground coriander
5 ml/1 tsp turmeric
A pinch of ground ginger
A pinch of chilli powder
1 large tomato, skinned and finely chopped
12 black peppercorns
50 g/2 oz/½ cup fresh or frozen peas
50 g/2 oz/½ cup fresh or frozen cranberries (optional)
30 ml/2 tbsp ghee
6 spring onions, finely chopped
5 ml/1 tsp cumin seeds, roasted and ground
120 ml/4 fl oz/½ cup soured cream

Method

1. Place the split peas and their soaking water in a large heavy-based saucepan and add the coriander, turmeric, ginger, chilli powder, tomato and peppercorns. Bring to the boil, cover and simmer for about 1½ hours until the split peas are tender.

2. Add the peas, cranberries, if using, and simmer for 3 minutes.

3. Heat the ghee in a small frying pan and fry the spring onions for 5 minutes until lightly browned. Add them to the soup with the cumin seeds and simmer for a further 5 minutes. Serve garnished with a spoonful of soured cream.

Serves 6

Salads

*Salads make delightful
accompaniments to Indian meals,
or any of these salads can be
served with a Western meal.
Onion salad is most commonly
found in British restaurants, and
it is often served with a starter or
with popadums.*

Onion Salad

Ingredients

4 large onions, sliced into thin rings
Salt and freshly ground black pepper
5 ml/1 tsp lemon juice

Method

1.   Soak the onion rings in water for at least 1 hour. This makes them a little less pungent.

2.   Just before serving, drain off the water thoroughly and season the onion rings with salt, freshly ground black pepper and lemon juice.

Serves 4

 # Carrot and Grape Salad

Ingredients

3 large carrots, cut into julienne strips
225 g/8 oz seedless grapes
30 ml/2 tbsp vegetable oil
15 ml/1 tbsp honey
15 ml/1 tbsp white wine vinegar
15 ml/1 tbsp lemon juice
5 ml/1 tsp mustard seeds, crushed
5 ml/1 tsp paprika
Freshly ground black pepper

Method

1.   Mix the carrots and grapes. Mix together all the

remaining ingredients, seasoning to taste with freshly ground black pepper. Pour over the salad and chill for 1 hour before serving.

Serves 4

3 Broccoli Salad

Ingredients

450 g/1 lb broccoli florets
45 ml/3 tbsp vegetable oil
2.5 cm/1 in piece ginger root, thinly sliced
100 g/4 oz button mushrooms
5 ml/1 tsp mustard seeds, crushed
2.5 ml/½ tsp chilli powder
4 cloves garlic, crushed
30 ml/2 tbsp lemon juice
5 ml/1 tsp honey
6 cherry tomatoes
Salt and freshly ground black pepper

Method

1. Bring a large saucepan of water to the boil, drop in the broccoli, bring back to the boil and boil for 1 minute. Drain thoroughly.

2. Heat the oil and fry the ginger and mushrooms for 1 minute. Add the mustard seeds, chilli powder and broccoli and fry for 2 minutes, stirring well. Leave to cool.

3. Mix the broccoli with the remaining ingredients and season to taste with salt and pepper. Chill for 1 hour before serving.

Serves 4 to 6

Breads
General Notes

Indian bread is served hot, within a few minutes of cooking, to accompany a meal. Traditionally the bread is torn into pieces and used to scoop up the meat and vegetable dishes.

Most breads are unleavened. In India they are cooked on a *tawa*, an iron griddle that is heated before the flat parathas or chappatis are slapped on to it. A heavy-based frying pan or griddle are adequate substitutes.

Naan bread contains yeast, but it can be made more quickly using baking powder as the raising agent. In India naan is baked in a clay oven called a tandoor. Bhatooras are deep-fried.

1 Bengal Parathas

Ingredients

225 g/8 oz/2 cups plain flour
2.5 ml/½ tsp salt
45 ml/3 tbsp ghee
120 ml/4 fl oz/½ cup water
Ghee for frying

Method

1. Mix together the flour and salt and rub in the ghee. Add the water and knead well for 10 minutes. Divide the dough into 12 equal portions.

2. Roll out the dough pieces into circles on a floured surface until as thin as possible. Fold in half and shape into triangles, then roll out again.

3. Heat a frying pan. Place the parathas two at a time in the dry pan and cook for 30 seconds on each side. Add 10 ml/2 tsp of ghee and continue to cook until the parathas have golden brown spots on both sides. Some parathas may rise more than others.

4. Serve piping hot with vegetable or meat dishes.

Makes 12

2   Chappatis

Ingredients

> 450 g/1 lb/4 cups wholewheat flour
> 2.5 ml/½ tsp salt
> 300 ml/½ pt/1 ¼ cups water
> 5 ml/1 tsp ghee

Method

1. Set aside a handful of flour for shaping the chappatis.

2. Mix the flour and salt and gradually knead in the water until you have a firm dough. Knead for at least 10 minutes.

3. Roll out the dough to a sausage shape about 20 cm/8 in long, cover and leave to stand for about 2 hours.

4. Just before serving your meal, knead and roll the dough again. Break off a small portion and roll it with a dash of ghee into a ball between your palms. Flatten the ball and roll out on a floured surface into a thin round pancake.

5. Heat a frying pan and add the chappati. Fry both sides, turning carefully and pressing down the chappati so that it rises like a balloon. Keep the chappatis warm while you fry the remainder.

6. Alternatively, bake the chappatis in a preheated oven at 180°C/350°F/gas mark 4 for about 3 minutes.

7. Serve the chappatis dry, or with a little ghee spread sparingly on one side.

Makes 12

3 | Yeast Naan

Ingredients

5 ml/1 tsp dried yeast or 10 ml/2 tsp fresh yeast
45 ml/3 tbsp warm water
5 ml/1 tsp sugar
450 g/1 lb/4 cups plain flour
5 ml/1 tsp salt
45 ml/3 tbsp vegetable oil
2 eggs, lightly beaten
450 ml/3/4 pt/2 cups natural yoghurt
30 ml/2 tbsp sesame or onion seeds

Method

1. Mix the yeast, water and sugar and leave to stand until the mixture becomes frothy.

2. Mix the flour, salt, vegetable oil and eggs. Add the yeast mixture and mix thoroughly. Add enough yoghurt to make a soft, elastic dough and knead well. Cover and leave in a warm place to rise for about 6 hours or until the dough has doubled in size.

3. Knead again and leave to stand for 10 minutes.

4. Divide the dough into about 12 pieces and roll each one out to a circle about the size of your palm. Traditionally naan are teardrop-shaped. You can achieve this by stretching one side slightly. Sprinkle with sesame or onion seeds.

5. Arrange the naans on greased baking sheets and bake in a preheated oven at 220°C/425°F/gas mark 7 for about 10 minutes until they are puffy and just beginning to turn brown. Serve hot.

Makes 12 to 15

4 | Quick Naan

Ingredients

450 g/1 lb/4 cups plain flour
450 ml/3/4 pt/2 cups natural yoghurt, lightly beaten
45 ml/3 tbsp vegetable oil
5 ml/1 tsp sugar
5 ml/1 tsp salt
2 eggs, lightly beaten
A pinch of baking powder
30 ml/2 tbsp sesame or onion seeds

Method

1. At least 3 hours before cooking, mix all the ingredients except the seeds to a smooth dough. Cover and leave to stand for 2 hours.

2. Roll out the naans to circles about the size of your palm. Traditionally they are teardrop-shaped. You can achieve this by stretching one side a little. Sprinkle with sesame or onion seeds.

3. Place the naans on greased baking sheets and cook in a preheated oven at 220°C/425°F/gas mark 7 for about 10 minutes until they are puffy and just beginning to turn brown.

Makes 12 to 15

5 | Bhatooras

Ingredients

350 g/12 oz/3 cups plain flour
2.5 ml/½ tsp baking powder
2.5 ml/½ tsp salt
250 ml/8 fl oz/1 cup natural yoghurt, lightly beaten
5 ml/1 tsp sugar
Vegetable oil for frying

Method

1. Sift the flour, baking powder and salt into a shallow bowl. Mix the yoghurt and sugar together and gradually add the mixture to the flour. Knead until you have a firm but not sticky dough. Cover and leave to stand in a warm place for 5 hours or overnight.

2. Cut the dough into about 15 pieces and roll them out into teardrop shapes, brushing with a little oil to prevent them sticking.

3. Heat the oil and fry the bhatooras a few at a time until they fluff up. Turn them over and cook for a few more seconds until the bhatoora is white flecked with brown. Remove from the pan and drain on kitchen paper.

Makes 15

Chicken
Curries

*In Indian cuisine, chicken can be
roasted and served in a tandoori-
style, served as a tikka dish,
made into curry or a biryani. The
skin is removed and the chicken
cut into small pieces or joints so
that the spices can penetrate
thoroughly into the flesh for the
most delicious flavours.*

1 Chicken Curry

Ingredients

1 medium chicken, skinned and cut into serving pieces
90 ml/6 tbsp natural yoghurt
2 onions, grated
2.5 ml/½ tsp grated ginger root
5 ml/1 tsp turmeric
A pinch of chilli powder
30 ml/2 tbsp ghee or vegetable oil
2 medium potatoes, peeled and halved
2.5 ml/½ tsp cumin seeds

Method

1. Mix the chicken pieces with the yoghurt, onions, ginger, turmeric and chilli powder. Leave to marinate for at least 30 minutes.

2. Heat the ghee or oil and fry the potatoes until golden brown. Remove from the pan and put to one side.

3. Fry the cumin seeds in the same oil for 2 minutes.

4. Pour the chicken and marinade into a flameproof casserole, mix in the cumin seeds and fry for 3 to 4 minutes. Arrange the potatoes over the chicken, cover and bake in a preheated oven at 160°C/ 325°F/gas mark 3 for about 1 hour until the chicken and potatoes are tender. Serve with rice.

5. If you prefer, you can add 250 ml/8 fl oz/1 cup of water to the chicken in step 4 and simmer over a low heat for about 1 hour until the chicken is cooked.

Serves 4 to 6

2 Chicken Dopiaza

Ingredients

60 ml/4 tbsp ghee
450 g/1 lb onions, sliced
750 g/1 ½ lb tomatoes, skinned and chopped
15 ml/1 tbsp ground coriander
15 ml/1 tbsp ground cumin
6 cloves garlic, crushed
6 dried red chillies, seeded and chopped
2.5 cm/1 in ginger root, grated
2.5 ml/½ tsp ground peppercorns
1 medium chicken, skinned and cut into serving pieces
2.5 ml/½ tsp ground saffron
600 ml/1 pt/2 ½ cups water
Salt
8 small new potatoes

Method

1. Heat the ghee and fry the onions until soft. Add the tomatoes, coriander, cumin, garlic, chillies, ginger and peppercorns and simmer, stirring, for about 15 minutes until thick.

2. Add the chicken and fry for 10 minutes.

3. Dissolve the saffron in a little water and add it to the pan with the remaining water. Season to taste with salt. Bring to the boil, cover and simmer for about 45 minutes until the chicken is almost tender.

4. Add the potatoes, cover and simmer for a further 15 minutes until the potatoes and chicken are cooked and a thick gravy remains.

Serves 4 to 6

3 Chicken Korma

Ingredients

4 large onions, sliced
6 green chillies, seeded
2.5 cm/1 in piece ginger root
Flesh of ¼ coconut
1 clove garlic
15 ml/1 tbsp poppy seeds
5 ml/1 tsp turmeric
15 ml/1 tbsp chopped fresh coriander
45 ml/3 tbsp ghee or vegetable oil
1 medium chicken, skinned and cut into serving pieces
1 cinnamon stick
2 cardamom pods
4 cloves
Salt
300 ml/½ pt/1 ¼ cups natural yoghurt
5 ml/1 tsp lemon juice

Method

1. Purée together 2 onions, the chillies, ginger, coconut, garlic, poppy seeds, turmeric and half the coriander to a smooth paste.

2. Heat the ghee or oil and fry the remaining onions until lightly browned. Add the paste and fry for 3 minutes.

3. Add the chicken and remaining spices, salt and yoghurt, cover and simmer gently for about 1 hour, adding a little water if necessary, until the chicken is tender. Season with lemon juice before serving.

Serves 4 to 6

4 Chicken Bhuna Masala

Ingredients

45 ml/3 tbsp vegetable oil
1 bay leaf
6 cardamoms
4 cloves
3 large onions, finely chopped
5 ml/1 tsp ground ginger
2.5 ml/½ tsp crushed garlic
3 large tomatoes, skinned and finely chopped
5 ml/1 tsp ground coriander
A pinch of turmeric
2 green chillies, seeded and chopped
Salt
1 small chicken, skinned and cut into serving pieces
60 ml/4 tbsp water
30 ml/2 tbsp finely chopped fresh coriander

Method

1. Heat the oil in a heavy-based saucepan and add the bay leaf. Peel and crush 4 of the cardamoms, add them to the pan with the cloves and fry for 3 seconds. Add the onions and fry until lightly browned, stirring continuously to prevent the onions sticking to the bottom of the pan.

2. Add the ginger and garlic and fry until golden brown. Add the tomatoes and continue to fry until the oil separates and comes to the top of the mixture. Add the ground coriander, turmeric, chillies and salt to taste and fry for a further 1 minute.

3.   Add the chicken pieces and stir to coat them with the mixture. Fry until the chicken is lightly browned, stirring frequently.

4.   Add the water, cover and cook over a low heat for about 40 minutes until the chicken is tender and the sauce has reduced to a thick clinging consistency.

5.   Peel and crush the remaining cardamoms. Sprinkle them over the pan, cover and cook for a further few minutes. Pour the curry into a warmed serving dish and serve sprinkled with the fresh coriander.

Serves 4 to 6

5 | Chicken Dhansak

Although this appears to have a lengthy list of ingredients, don't let it put you off as there is nothing complicated about the recipe.

Ingredients

1 small chicken, skinned and cut into serving pieces
45 ml/3 tbsp split peas, soaked overnight and drained
45 ml/3 tbsp green lentils, soaked overnight and drained
45 ml/3 tbsp red lentils, soaked overnight and drained
1 aubergine, chopped
2 courgettes, chopped
2 potatoes, cubed
2 onions, chopped
2.5 ml/½ tsp turmeric
Salt
60 ml/4 tbsp vegetable oil
3 spring onions, chopped
2.5 ml/½ tsp fenugreek seeds
5 ml/1 tsp ground cumin
10 ml/2 tsp ground coriander
10 ml/2 tsp ground ginger
6 cloves garlic, crushed
25 g/1 oz tamarind pods, soaked in water (optional)

Method

1.   Put the chicken, pulses, vegetables, turmeric and salt to taste in a heavy-based saucepan. Add enough water just to cover the ingredients, bring to the boil, cover and simmer for about 1 hour until the chicken and pulses are tender.

2.   Remove from the heat and take out the chicken pieces. Purée the remaining ingredients then return everything to the saucepan.

3. Heat the oil in a second saucepan and fry the spring onions until golden brown. Remove half of them and reserve them for garnish. Add the fenugreek seeds to the pan and fry for a few minutes. As soon as they stop spluttering, add the cumin, coriander, ginger and garlic and fry for a few minutes, stirring, and adding a teaspoon or so of water if necessary. Pour over the chicken.

4. Bring the chicken mixture to the boil, cover and simmer.

5. Meanwhile, press the tamarind seeds through a strainer, if using, and add to the chicken with the strained soaking water. Simmer for 10 minutes or until the curry has thickened. Serve garnished with the reserved onions.

6. As a variation, you can substitute lamb for chicken. This will take about 1½ hours to cook and you will need to add a little more water during cooking.

7. If you use a pressure cooker, the dish will cook in just 20 minutes once the cooker has reached maximum pressure.

Serves 6 to 8

7 Chicken Moghlai

Ingredients

45 ml/3 tbsp vegetable oil
3 onions, sliced
60 ml/4 tbsp natural yoghurt
60 ml/4 tbsp double cream
1 small chicken, skinned and cut into serving pieces
5 cardamoms, peeled and crushed
7 cloves garlic, crushed
25 cashew nuts, ground to a paste
2 green chillies, seeded and chopped
Juice of 1 lime
15 ml/1 tbsp chopped fresh coriander

Method

1. Heat the oil in a heavy-based saucepan and fry the onions until golden brown.

2. Lightly beat the yoghurt and cream and mix in the chicken, cardamoms, garlic, nuts and chillies.

3. Add the chicken mixture to the pan, cover and simmer gently for about 1 hour until the chicken is tender and the sauce has thickened to the consistency you like. Stir in the lime juice and serve sprinkled with coriander.

Serves 4 to 6

7 | Kashmir Chicken with Nuts

Ingredients

45 ml/3 tbsp vegetable oil
2 large onions, thinly sliced
1 cinnamon stick
4 cloves
3 cardamoms, peeled and crushed
1 medium chicken, skinned and cut into serving pieces
8 almonds, thinly sliced
8 cashew nuts, sliced lengthways
15 ml/1 tbsp raisins
45 ml/3 tbsp double cream, lightly beaten
250 ml/8 fl oz/1 cup natural yoghurt, lightly beaten
A few strands saffron, soaked in the yoghurt
15 ml/1 tbsp finely chopped fresh coriander
1 green chilli, seeded and chopped

Method

1. Heat the oil and fry the onions until lightly browned. Add the cinnamon, cloves and cardamoms and fry for 1 minute.

2. Add the chicken pieces and fry until lightly browned all over.

3. Just cover the chicken with cold water, bring to the boil, cover and simmer gently for about 40 minutes until the chicken is tender and the liquid has evaporated.

4. Add the nuts, raisins, cream and yoghurt and heat through gently without allowing the sauce to boil. Serve garnished with the fresh coriander and chilli.

Serves 4 to 6

8 | Chicken Sagwala

Ingredients

60 ml/4 tbsp vegetable oil
3 cloves
2.5 cm/1 in piece cinnamon stick
2 cardamoms, peeled and crushed
4 onions, finely chopped
15 ml/1 tbsp ground ginger
1 clove garlic, crushed
2 green chillies, seeded and chopped
4 large tomatoes, skinned and chopped
A pinch of turmeric
10 ml/2 tsp ground coriander
Salt
1 small chicken, skinned and cut into serving pieces
450 g/1 lb spinach, finely chopped
120 ml/4 fl oz/½ cup water

Method

1. Heat the oil in a heavy-based saucepan. Add the cloves, cinnamon and cardamoms and fry for a few seconds. Add the onions and fry until they are lightly browned.

2. Mix together the ginger and garlic and add it to the pan, stirring continuously, and keep frying until the mixture is a rich golden brown. Add a few teaspoons of water if necessary.

3. Add the chillies and tomatoes and continue cooking until the oil begins to separate and rise to the top of the mixture.

4. Add the turmeric, coriander and salt to taste and cook for a further 1 minute. Add the chicken and fry until lightly browned all over.

5. Add the spinach, stir well, cover and simmer for 20 minutes. Add the water, cover again and simmer for a further 15 minutes until the chicken is cooked through and the sauce is thick and clinging to the chicken pieces.

6. As a variation, you can use lamb instead of chicken and cook for about 1 hour.

7. If you use a pressure cooker, the dish will cook in about 20 minutes after the cooker has reached maximum pressure. Add about 120 ml/4 fl oz/½ cup of water before you close the cooker.

Serves 6 to 8

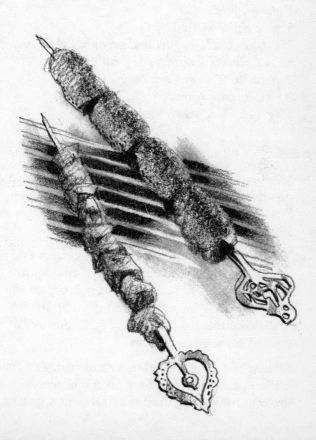

9 Chicken Tikka Masala

Ingredients

20 ml/1 ½ tbsp lime juice
5 ml/1 tsp ground ginger
1 clove garlic, crushed
5 ml/1 tsp chilli powder
Salt and freshly ground black pepper
10 boned chicken breasts, cubed
45 ml/3 tbsp vegetable oil
1 bay leaf
2.5 cm/1 in piece cinnamon stick
3 onions, finely sliced
5 ml/1 tsp turmeric
250 ml/8 fl oz/1 cup natural yoghurt, lightly beaten
30 ml/2 tbsp finely chopped fresh coriander
1 green chilli, seeded and chopped
2.5 ml/½ tsp sugar
25 g/1 oz blanched almonds, sliced

Method

1. Mix together the lime juice, ginger, garlic and chilli powder and season to taste with salt and pepper. Rub the mixture well into the chicken, cover and leave to marinate for 2 hours.

2. Thread the chicken pieces on to skewers and arrange on a rack in a baking tin lined with kitchen foil so that the juices can drain off the skewers. Cook in a preheated oven at 180°C/350°F/gas mark 4 for about 15 minutes until cooked through and crisp.

3. Meanwhile, heat the oil in a saucepan, add the bay leaf and cinnamon and fry for a few seconds. Add the onions and fry until they are a rich golden

brown, stirring frequently so that they do not burn.

4. Add the turmeric and fry for a few seconds then remove from the heat and add the yoghurt, coriander, chilli and sugar. Stir vigorously to mix all the ingredients then return the pan to the heat, cover and simmer over a low heat for about 10 minutes until the sauce thickens.

5. Add the cooked tikkas and simmer for a further 10 minutes until they have absorbed the flavours of the gravy. Serve garnished with almonds.

Serves 4 to 6

10 Murgh Makhani

This is a popular speciality from northern India. It is rich (in calories as well as taste), creamy and quite irresistible.

Ingredients

30 ml/2 tbsp sour yoghurt, lightly beaten
Juice of 2 limes
1 clove garlic, crushed
10 ml/2 tsp ground ginger
5 ml/1 tsp chilli powder
5 ml/1 tsp ground coriander
Salt
1 small chicken, skinned and cut into serving pieces
30 ml/2 tbsp vegetable oil
450 g/1 lb tomatoes, skinned and chopped
30 ml/2 tbsp chopped fresh coriander
5 cm/2 in piece ginger root, chopped
1 green chilli, seeded and chopped
A pinch of turmeric
15 ml/1 tbsp tomato ketchup (optional)
5 ml/1 tsp sugar
Freshly ground black pepper
450 ml/¾ pt/2 cups cream
2.5 ml/½ tsp garam masala
2.5 ml/½ tsp ground cumin

Method

1. Mix together the yoghurt, lime juice, garlic, ginger, chilli, coriander and salt to make a marinade. Make gashes or prick holes all over the chicken pieces and rub in the marinade. Cover and leave to marinate overnight.

2.   Heat the oil in a heavy-based saucepan, add the chicken and marinade and bring to the boil. Cover and simmer over a low heat for about 30 minutes until all the moisture has evaporated.

3.   Meanwhile, purée together all the remaining ingredients except the cream, garam masala and cumin.

4.   Pour the purée into a saucepan. Lightly beat half the cream and stir it into the puréed mixture. Heat over a low heat until the fat separates.

5.   Add the chicken pieces to the sauce and cook over a low heat until the chicken is cooked through.

6.   Just before serving, gently stir in the remaining cream and sprinkle with the garam masala and cumin.

Serves 4

11 | Chicken Madras

Madras is a hot curry from southern India. The spices in this recipe are more subtle than those used in Meat Madras in order not to overpower the more delicate flavour of the chicken.

Ingredients

1 medium chicken, skinned and cut into serving pieces
1 lemon
10 ml/2 tsp chilli powder
10 ml/2 tsp black pepper
5 ml/1 tsp salt
60 ml/4 tbsp vegetable oil or ghee
2 large onions, finely chopped
3 cloves garlic, crushed
5 cm/2 in piece ginger root, finely chopped
20 ml/4 tsp ground cumin
10 ml/2 tsp ground coriander
5 ml/1 tsp turmeric
1 green chilli, seeded and chopped
2 bay leaves
600 ml/1 pt/2 ½ cups boiling water
10 ml/2 tsp garam masala

Method

1. Make a couple of cuts in each chicken piece. Put the pieces in a bowl and squeeze over the lemon juice.

2. Mix together the chilli powder, pepper and salt and sprinkle over the chicken. Cover and leave to marinate for at least 2 hours.

3. Heat the oil or ghee in a heavy-based saucepan and fry the onion, garlic and ginger over a low

heat until soft. Stir in the cumin, coriander and turmeric and cook for a further 2 minutes. Add the chilli, chicken and marinade and fry the chicken on all sides.

4. Add the bay leaves and boiling water, bring to the boil, cover and simmer for 45 minutes.

5. Add the garam masala, stir well and cook for a further 15 minutes until the chicken is tender and falls away from the bones.

Serves 6

12 | Chicken Pal

The fiery red sauce of this curry is as hot as it looks. You can decrease or increase the hotness by varying the amount of chillies and chilli powder used. This curry is only for those who like their curry really hot.

Ingredients

45 ml/3 tbsp vegetable oil or ghee
1 onion, finely chopped
8 cloves garlic, crushed
5 cm/2 in piece ginger root, finely chopped
15 ml/1 tbsp chilli powder
5 ml/1 tsp ground cumin
5 ml/1 tsp ground coriander
2.5 ml/½ tsp ground fenugreek
5 ml/1 tsp garam masala
400 g/14 oz tin tomatoes
30 ml/2 tbsp tomato purée
12 green chillies, seeded and chopped
1 small chicken, skinned and cut into serving pieces
Salt

Method

1. Heat half the oil in a heavy-based saucepan and fry the onion, cloves and ginger until soft.

2. Mix the chilli powder, cumin, coriander, fenugreek and garam masala with a little water to make a smooth paste. Stir this into the onion mixture and cook over a low heat for 10 minutes.

3. Add the tomatoes, tomato purée and chillies and cook for a further 10 minutes.

4.   In another pan, heat the remaining oil or ghee and fry the chicken pieces until golden brown.

5.   Place all the ingredients in a casserole dish and season to taste with salt. Cook in a preheated oven at 200°C/400°F/gas mark 6 for 1 hour or until the chicken is tender.

6.   As a variation, a good cut of lamb or beef can be substituted for the chicken. Fry the meat until brown before adding it to the other ingredients. Prawns can also be used for this recipe but will require a shorter cooking time.

Serves 4

13 Punjab Butter Chicken

Ingredients

60 ml/4 tbsp natural yoghurt, lightly beaten
Juice of 1 lime
1 clove garlic, crushed
10 ml/2 tsp ground ginger
5 ml/1 tsp chilli powder
5 ml/1 tsp ground coriander
Salt
1 medium chicken, skinned and cut into serving pieces
30 ml/2 tbsp vegetable oil
5 large tomatoes, skinned and chopped
30 ml/2 tbsp chopped fresh coriander
2.5 cm/1 in piece ginger root, chopped
2 green chillies, seeded and chopped
A pinch of turmeric
15 ml/1 tbsp tomato sauce (optional)
5 ml/1 tsp sugar
Salt and freshly ground black pepper
175 ml/6 fl oz/¾ cup cream
2.5 ml/½ tsp garam masala
2.5 ml/½ tsp ground cumin

Method

1. Mix together the yoghurt, lime juice, garlic, ginger, chilli powder, ground coriander and salt.

2. Make gashes or prick holes all over the chicken and rub in the marinade. Cover and leave to stand for as long as possible, preferably overnight.

3. Heat the oil, add the chicken and marinade and fry over a gentle heat for about 30 minutes until the chicken is tender and the liquid has evaporated.

4. Meanwhile, purée together the tomatoes, fresh coriander, ginger, chillies, turmeric, tomato sauce, if using, sugar, salt and pepper. Lightly beat half the cream and stir it into the mixture with a little water.

5. Heat the sauce over a low heat, stirring occasionally, until the fat rises to the top. Taste and adjust the seasoning if necessary.

6. Add the chicken to the sauce and heat it through gently.

7. Just before serving, stir in the remaining cream and serve sprinkled with garam masala and cumin.

Serves 4

14 Chicken Vindaloo

Ingredients

5-10 ml/1-2 tsp chilli powder
5 ml/1 tsp turmeric
10 ml/2 tsp ground cumin
10 ml/2 tsp ground mustard seeds
4 cm/1 ½ in piece ginger root, finely chopped
Salt
150 ml/¼ pt/⅔ cup white wine vinegar
1 large onion, finely chopped
2 cloves garlic, crushed
1 small chicken, skinned and cut into serving pieces
60 ml/4 tbsp vegetable oil or ghee

Method

1. Mix together the spices and salt to taste with the wine vinegar.

2. Put the onion, garlic and chicken pieces into a bowl, pour over the spiced vinegar, cover and leave to marinate overnight.

3. Heat the oil or ghee in a heavy-based saucepan and add the chicken and marinade. Bring to the boil, cover and simmer for 45 minutes until the chicken is tender.

4. As a variation, you can substitute prawns instead of chicken and reduce the cooking time slightly.

Serves 4

Meat Curries

General Notes

Lamb is the most popular meat in India. Pork is not eaten by Muslims for religious reasons. Beef is not eaten by Hindus, and it is also not of a particularly good quality. However, most of the recipes in this chapter could be prepared equally well with a good cut of beef.

Indian dishes require lean meat, so any fat should be trimmed off before cooking. Leg of lamb is ideal. Either cut the meat from the bone yourself, or ask the butcher to do it for you.

Meat is often marinated overnight in yoghurt and spices to tenderise it and allow the flavours to penetrate the meat.

1 | Lamb Curry

Ingredients

1 kg/2 lb leg of lamb, boned and cubed
2 onions, finely chopped
2 cloves garlic, crushed
15 ml/1 tbsp grated ginger root
250 ml/8 fl oz/1 cup natural yoghurt
5 ml/1 tsp turmeric
5 ml/1 tsp paprika
5 ml/1 tsp ground cumin
2.5 ml/½ tsp chilli powder
15 ml/1 tbsp mustard oil (optional)
30 ml/2 tbsp vegetable oil
30 ml/2 tbsp ghee
10 ml/2 tsp salt
2.5 ml/½ tsp sugar
500 ml/18 fl oz/2 cups water
2 cardamoms, peeled and crushed

Method

1.   Mix together the meat, onions, garlic, ginger, yoghurt, turmeric, paprika, cumin, chilli powder and mustard oil, if using. Cover and marinate for at least 2 hours.

2.   Heat the oil and ghee in a heavy-based saucepan and add the meat and marinade, stirring well. Bring to the boil, cover and simmer over a medium heat for about 15 minutes until the moisture has evaporated.

3.   Add the salt, sugar and water, bring to the boil, cover and simmer for about 1 hour until the meat is tender. Serve sprinkled with cardamoms.

4.   As a variation, you can use a good cut of beef for this recipe.

Serves 4 to 6

2 Sag Ghosht

Ingredients

1 kg/2 lb leg of lamb, boned and cubed
5 ml/1 tsp turmeric
250 ml/8 fl oz/1 cup water
45 ml/3 tbsp vegetable oil
45 ml/3 tbsp ghee
2 cardamoms, peeled and crushed
1 cinnamon stick, broken into pieces
4 onions, finely chopped
2 cloves garlic, crushed
10 ml/2 tsp grated ginger root
90 ml/6 tbsp natural yoghurt
5 ml/1 tsp sugar
10 ml/2 tsp salt
225 g/8 oz cooked spinach

Method

1. Mix together the meat, turmeric and water in a heavy-based saucepan. Bring to the boil, cover and simmer for about 1 hour until the meat is tender.

2. Heat the oil and ghee. Add the cardamoms, cinnamon, onions and garlic and cook for 5 minutes, stirring occasionally. Add the ginger and stir well.

3. Add the meat, yoghurt, sugar and salt and cook for 5 minutes.

4. Add the spinach and cook for a further 15 minutes, stirring occasionally.

5. As a variation, you can substitute beef for the lamb.

Serves 4 to 6

3 Korma Curry

Ingredients

1 kg/2 lb leg of lamb, boned and cubed
5 ml/1 tsp turmeric
375 ml/13 fl oz/1 ½ cups water
60 ml/4 tbsp vegetable oil
60 ml/4 tbsp ghee
2 small turnips, diced
4 onions, thinly sliced
30 ml/2 tbsp grated ginger root
3 cloves garlic, crushed
10 ml/2 tsp sugar
5 ml/1 tsp chilli powder
75 ml/5 tbsp natural yoghurt
50 g/2 oz shelled peas, fresh or frozen
Salt

Method

1. Place the lamb, turmeric and water in a heavy-based saucepan, bring to the boil, cover and simmer for about 1 hour until the meat is tender. Drain the meat and keep the meat and liquid to one side.

2. Heat the oil and ghee and fry the turnips for about 5 minutes, then remove from the pan and drain on kitchen paper.

3. Fry the onions until golden brown. Add the ginger, garlic, sugar and chilli powder and fry gently for 2 minutes. Add the meat and fry for 3 minutes. Add the yoghurt and liquid from the meat and heat gently.

4. Add the peas and turnips and season to taste with salt. Cover and simmer until the turnips are soft.

5. As a variation, you could use beef for this recipe.

Serves 4 to 6

4 Minced Meat with Peas

Ingredients

45 ml/3 tbsp vegetable oil
1 clove garlic, thinly sliced
2 onions, thinly sliced
450 g/1 lb minced meat
5 ml/1 tsp turmeric
2.5 ml/½ tsp ground cinnamon
2.5 ml/½ tsp paprika
A pinch of chilli powder
15 ml/1 tbsp natural yoghurt
10 ml/2 tsp salt
2.5 ml/½ tsp sugar
100 g/4 oz/1 cup frozen peas

Method

1. Heat the oil in a heavy-based saucepan and fry the garlic until lightly browned. Add the onion and fry until golden brown.

2. Add the meat, turmeric, cinnamon, paprika and chilli powder and mix well. Add the yoghurt, salt and sugar and fry over a medium heat for about 5 minutes, stirring occasionally.

3. Add the peas, cover and simmer over a medium heat for about 30 minutes until the meat is tender.

Serves 4

5 | Bhuna Ghosht

Ingredients

375 ml/13 fl oz/1 ½ cups natural yoghurt
5 ml/1 tsp ground ginger
6 cloves garlic, crushed
6 cardamoms, peeled and crushed
½ cinnamon stick, broken into pieces
5 ml/1 tsp ground cloves
450 g/1 lb leg of lamb, boned and cubed
45 ml/3 tbsp vegetable oil
3 large onions, sliced
5 ml/1 tsp ground coriander
5 ml/1 tsp ground aniseed
A pinch of turmeric
Salt and freshly ground black pepper
120 ml/4 fl oz/½ cup water
15 ml/1 tbsp finely chopped fresh coriander

Method

1. Lightly beat 15 ml/1 tbsp of the yoghurt with the ginger, garlic, cardamoms, cinnamon and cloves. Rub the mixture well into the pieces of meat and leave to marinate for 2 hours.

2. Heat the oil in a heavy-based saucepan and fry the onions until golden brown. Remove the onions from the oil and keep to one side.

3. Add the meat to the pan and fry until lightly browned all over.

4. Add the fried onions to the remaining yoghurt with the ground coriander, aniseed and turmeric and season to taste with salt and pepper.

5.   Add this mixture to the meat, stir well, add the water, cover and simmer for about 1 hour until the meat is tender and the liquid has evaporated. Serve garnished with fresh coriander.

6.   If you use a pressure cooker, omit the water. The dish will cook in about 25 minutes after the cooker has reached maximum pressure.

Serves **4**

6 Lamb and Coconut Curry

Ingredients

406 ml/18 fl oz/2 cups hot water
1 small coconut, grated
60 ml/4 tbsp vegetable oil
6 cloves
A pinch of asafoetida
5 ml/1 tsp mustard seeds
10 curry leaves
2 green chillies, seeded and chopped
3 large onions, chopped
5 ml/1 tsp ground coriander
5 ml/1 tsp poppy seeds, roasted and ground
3 cardamoms, peeled and crushed
900 g/2 lb leg of lamb, boned and cubed
15 ml/1 tbsp finely chopped fresh coriander

Method

1. Pour the hot water over the coconut in a bowl and leave to stand.

2. Heat the oil and fry the cloves for a few seconds. Add the asafoetida and fry until it stops fizzing. Add the mustard seeds and fry until they stop spluttering. Add the curry leaves and chillies and fry for a few seconds. Add the onions and fry until golden brown.

3. Add the ground coriander, poppy seeds and cardamoms and fry for 1 minute.

4. Add the meat and mix to coat it well with the spices. Fry until it is well browned all over.

5. Drain the coconut, reserving the liquid, and press down to extract as much flavour as possible. Pour the liquid over the meat and add a few coconut shreds. Bring to the boil, cover and simmer for about 1 hour until the lamb is tender and the sauce is the consistency you prefer. You may need to add a little more water during the cooking process.

6. Stir well and serve garnished with the fresh coriander.

    Serves 6 to 8

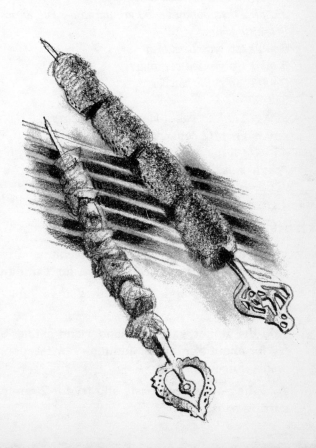

7 | Lamb Pasanda

Ingredients

45 ml/3 tbsp vegetable oil
1 cinnamon stick
3 cloves
2 cardamoms, peeled and crushed
4 onions, finely chopped
15 ml/1 tbsp ground ginger
1 clove garlic, crushed
30 ml/2 tbsp finely chopped fresh coriander
2 green chillies, seeded and chopped
75 ml/5 tbsp poppy seeds, ground to a paste with
   a little water
5 ml/1 tsp ground cumin
5 ml/1 tsp ground coriander
5 ml/1 tsp chilli powder
Salt
900 g/2 lb lean boned lamb, cut into strips
450 ml/¾ pt/2 cups water
45 ml/3 tbsp cashew nuts, ground to a paste with a
   little milk
120 ml/4 fl oz/½ cup double cream, lightly beaten
2 green chillies, seeded and sliced (optional)

Method

1. Heat the oil in a heavy-based saucepan and fry the cinnamon, cloves and cardamoms for 1 minute.

2. Add the onions and fry until they are a light pinkish colour.

3. Add the ginger, garlic, coriander and chillies and fry for about 5 minutes, adding a few teaspoons of water if necessary.

4. Add the poppy seed paste and fry for 2 minutes, stirring constantly.

5.   Add the cumin, coriander and chilli powder and season to taste with salt. Fry for 1 minute.

6.   Add the meat to the pan and fry lightly until just browned. Add the water, bring to the boil, cover and simmer for about 1 hour until the meat is tender and all the liquid has evaporated.

7.   Just before serving, add the cashew paste and cream and heat through gently without boiling. Serve garnished with green chillies, if using.

Serves 6 to 8

8 Lamb Dopiaza

Ingredients

60 ml/4 tbsp vegetable oil
2 cardamoms, peeled and crushed
3 cloves
2.5 cm/1 in piece cinnamon stick
3 onions, finely chopped
10 ml/2 tsp ground ginger
1 clove garlic, crushed
3 large tomatoes, skinned and chopped
2 green chillies, seeded and chopped
2.5 ml/½ tsp ground fenugreek
5 ml/1 tsp ground coriander
A pinch of turmeric
Salt
450 g/1 lb lean boned lamb, cut into chunks
450 ml/¾ pt/2 cups water
2 onions, sliced into rings
30 ml/2 tbsp finely chopped fresh coriander
2.5 ml/½ tsp garam masala

Method

1.   Heat the oil in a heavy-based saucepan and fry the cardamoms, cloves and cinnamon until they stop fizzing. Add the onions and fry until browned, stirring continuously.

2.   Add the ginger and garlic and fry until golden brown, stirring to make sure they do not stick to the bottom and adding a little water if necessary.

3.   Add the tomatoes, chillies, fenugreek, ground coriander and turmeric and season to taste with salt. Fry for 1 minute.

4. Add the meat and fry lightly until the juices run. Add the water, cover and cook over a low heat for about 1 hour until the meat is tender and the liquid has evaporated.

5. Add the onion rings, fresh coriander and garam masala, stir well and simmer for a further 10 minutes before serving.

6. If you use a pressure cooker add only 250 ml/ 8 fl oz/1 cup of water and cook for 25 minutes after the cooker has reached maximum pressure.

Serves 4

9 Rogan Josh

Ingredients

45 ml/3 tbsp vegetable oil
A large pinch of asafoetida
3 cloves
2.5 cm/1 in piece cinnamon stick
3 cardamoms, peeled and crushed
5 ml/1 tsp black peppercorns
30 ml/2 tbsp sugar
900 g/2 lb lean lamb or beef, boned and cubed
15 ml/1 tbsp ground ginger
450 ml/¾ pt/2 cups natural yoghurt, lightly beaten
2 large tomatoes, skinned and chopped
5 ml/1 tsp chilli powder
5 ml/1 tsp ground coriander
Salt
450-750 ml/¾ to 1¼ pts/2-3 cups water
15 ml/1 tbsp butter (optional)
15 ml/1 tbsp finely chopped fresh coriander

Method

1. Heat the oil in a heavy-based saucepan and fry the asafoetida until it has darkened and stopped fizzing. Add the cloves, cinnamon, cardamoms and peppercorns and fry for 1 minute.

2. Add the sugar and stir over a low heat until it turns golden brown and caramelises. Be careful not to let it burn.

3. Add the meat and cook until the juices have evaporated.

4. Add the ginger and fry until lightly browned. Add the yoghurt, tomatoes, chilli powder and ground

coriander and season to taste with salt. Cook, stirring frequently, until the yoghurt is absorbed.

5.   Add the water, using 450 ml/¾ pt/2 cups if you do not want a sauce at the end, a little more if you like a thick sauce or more still if you like a thinnish curry. Cover and simmer over a low heat for about 1 hour until the meat is tender and the gravy is the consistency you like.

6.   Stir in the butter, if using, and serve garnished with fresh coriander.

7.   If you use a pressure cooker, add 250 ml/8 fl oz/1 cup of water if you want no sauce, 375 ml/13 fl oz/1 ½ cups for a thick sauce or 450 ml/¾ pt/ 2 cups for a thin sauce. Cook for 35 minutes after the cooker has reached maximum pressure.

Serves 4 to 6

10 Kashmir Lamb Curry

This is a sweet-tasting and fairly mild curry.

Ingredients

900 g/2 lb leg of lamb, boned and cubed
250 ml/8 fl oz/1 cup natural yoghurt
5 ml/1 tsp turmeric
5 ml/1 tsp ground cumin
2.5 ml/½ tsp chilli powder
3 cloves garlic, crushed
45 ml/3 tbsp vegetable oil or ghee
50 g/2 oz/¼ cup flaked almonds
75 g/3 oz/½ cup sultanas
50 g/2 oz/⅓ cup thinly sliced dried apricots
Juice of 1 lemon
Salt

Method

1. Place the lamb in a bowl. Mix together the yoghurt, turmeric, cumin, chilli powder and garlic and mix it into the meat. Cover and leave to marinate in the refrigerator for several hours or overnight if possible.

2. Heat the oil or ghee and fry the flaked almonds for 2 minutes. Remove them from the pan and drain on kitchen paper.

3. Fry the sultanas and apricots until they become plump. Remove them from the pan and drain on kitchen paper.

4.   Add the lamb and marinade to the pan and fry for
     5 minutes until browned. Add the almonds,
     sultanas and apricots, cover and simmer gently for
     1 hour, stirring occasionally, until the meat is
     tender.

5.   Stir in the lemon juice and season to taste with
     salt.

6.   As a variation, you can substitute beef or prawns
     in this recipe.

Serves 4 to 6

11 | Meat Madras

This is a fairly dry dish from southern India and is flavoured with coconut and curry leaves. It is quite a hot curry.

Ingredients

60 ml/4 tbsp vegetable oil or ghee
2 onions, chopped
450 g/1 lb lean lamb or beef, cubed
150 ml/¼ pt/⅔ cup water
2.5 cm/1 in piece cinnamon stick
10 black peppercorns
3 cloves
15 ml/1 tbsp coriander seeds
2.5 ml/½ tsp chilli powder
50 g/2 oz/½ cup desiccated coconut
6 curry leaves
2.5 ml/½ tsp turmeric
Salt

Method

1. Heat 45 ml/3 tbsp of the oil or ghee in a heavy-based saucepan and fry half the onion until lightly browned. Add the meat and water, bring to the boil, cover and simmer for 30 minutes or until the meat is fairly tender.

2. In a separate saucepan, dry roast the cinnamon, peppercorns, cloves, coriander seeds and chilli powder over a low heat for a few seconds. Leave to cool, then grind them to a paste.

3. Heat the remaining oil or ghee and fry the remaining onion. Add the coconut and curry leaves then the turmeric, ground spices and

cooked meat mixture. Season to taste with salt. Cover and simmer gently for about 30 minutes until the meat is tender and the sauce has thickened, adding a little extra water if necessary.

Serves 4

12 Meat Pal

Follow the recipe for Chicken Pal on page 68 but substitute 450 g/1 lb lean lamb or beef for the chicken.

13 Lamb Dhansak

Follow the recipe for Chicken Dhansak on page 56 but substitute 450 g/1 lb lean lamb or beef for the chicken.

14 Lamb Vindaloo

Ingredients

2 onions, chopped
4 cloves garlic, crushed
2.5 cm/1 in piece ginger root, crushed
2.5 cm/1 in piece cinnamon stick
4 cloves
6 black peppercorns
5 ml/1 tsp cumin seeds
5 ml/1 tsp mustard seeds
120 ml/4 fl oz/½ cup white wine vinegar
900 g/2 lb leg of lamb, boned and cubed
45 ml/3 tbsp vegetable oil or ghee
450 g/1 lb tomatoes, skinned and chopped
5 ml/1 tsp turmeric
Salt
15 ml/1 tbsp chopped fresh coriander

Method

1. Grind the onions, garlic, ginger, cinnamon, cloves, peppercorns, cumin seeds and mustard seeds with a little wine vinegar to a thick paste.

2. Rub the mixture well into the pieces of meat, cover and leave to marinate for at least 1 hour.

3. Heat the oil or ghee in a heavy-based saucepan and add the meat and marinade, the tomatoes and turmeric. Stir well until the tomatoes are broken up. Add the remaining vinegar and season to taste with salt. Cover and simmer gently for about 1 hour until the meat is tender. Serve garnished with fresh coriander.

Serves 4 to 6

Balti Dishes

General Notes

Balti dishes are brought to the table sizzling in a *balti* or wok. The baltis are heated until they are really hot and then cooked curry is poured in. As the moisture meets the hot base of the pan, there is an aromatic sizzling that sets your taste buds tingling.

The two recipes given here are quite different from each other. The chicken is sautéed and then dunked into the sauce to complete the cooking. The meat, however, is cooked along with the spices and onions and the prepared curry is then poured into the balti before it is served.

Balti dishes often have pieces of vegetable — onion, tomato, pepper, potato — in the curry. The vegetables are usually fried separately before they are added to the curry. Onions, tomatoes and peppers only take a few minutes, but potatoes take longer to cook. If you are short of time, they can be parboiled before they are fried. Potatoes would be a good addition to the meat recipes given here.

As well as the two recipes in this chapter, you could try almost any other curry sauce, apart from cream-based sauces which may not be able to take the extra heat.

For an extra special finishing touch to your balti dish, here's something you can try. After heating the balti, and just before pouring in the meat or chicken curry, drop in a pinch of spice — cumin, crushed cardamom, cinnamon, aniseed —let it roast lightly, and then pour in the curry. The aroma of the freshly roasted spice is quite delightful.

1 Balti Chicken

Ingredients

45 ml/3 tbsp vegetable oil
1 medium chicken, skinned and cut into serving pieces
6 cardamoms
450 g/1 lb tomatoes, skinned and chopped
1 large green pepper, chopped
2 green chillies, seeded and chopped
A pinch of turmeric
5 ml/1 tsp sugar
2.5 ml/½ tsp freshly ground black pepper
Salt
250 ml/8 fl oz/1 cup water
2.5 cm/1 in piece cinnamon stick (optional)

Method

1. Heat the oil in a heavy-based frying pan and fry the chicken pieces until lightly browned. Remove them from the oil and put to one side.

2. Add the cardamoms to the pan and fry for 2 minutes.

3. Purée the tomatoes and pepper and place in a saucepan. Add the cardamoms, chillies, turmeric, sugar and pepper and season to taste with salt. Bring to the boil, cover and simmer over a low heat, stirring occasionally, until the oil rises to the top.

4. Add the chicken pieces and water, bring back to the boil, cover and simmer for about 45 minutes until the chicken is tender and the sauce is the thickness you prefer.

5. When you are ready to serve, heat a large balti dish or individual ones and test whether they are hot enough by dropping in a teaspoonful of water. It should start sizzling immediately. Drop in the cinnamon stick, if using.

6. Pour in the chicken curry and serve at once.

Serves 4 to 6

2 Balti Meat

Ingredients

45 ml/3 tbsp vegetable oil
1 bay leaf
3 cloves
2 cardamoms, peeled and crushed
3 large onions, finely chopped
5 ml/1 tsp ground ginger
1 clove garlic, crushed
3 large tomatoes, skinned and puréed
A pinch of turmeric
10 ml/2 tsp ground coriander
2.5 ml/½ tsp ground cumin
2 green chillies, seeded and chopped
450 g/1 lb lamb or beef, cubed
Salt
30 ml/2 tbsp finely chopped fresh coriander

Method

1. Heat the oil in a heavy-based saucepan and fry the bay leaf, cloves and cardamoms for 1 minute. Add the onions and fry until lightly browned, stirring continuously to prevent them sticking to the bottom of the pan.

2. Add the ginger and garlic and continue to cook, stirring, until the mixture is a rich golden brown, adding a little water if the mixture begins to stick to the bottom.

3. Add the tomatoes and cook until the oil rises to the top. Add the turmeric, ground coriander, cumin and chillies and fry for 1 minute.

4. Add the meat and season to taste with salt. Fry until lightly browned, adding a little water if necessary to prevent the meat sticking.

5. Add enough water to cover the meat, cover and simmer for about 1 hour until the meat is tender and the sauce is the consistency you prefer.

6. When you are ready to serve, heat a large balti or individual ones. Test whether it is hot enough by dropping in a teaspoonful of water. It should start sizzling immediately.

7. Pour in the meat curry and serve immediately, garnished with fresh coriander.

8. If you are using a pressure cooker, reduce the amount of water. Cook for 25 minutes after the cooker reaches maximum pressure.

Serves 4

Seafood Curries

General Notes

Fish and seafoods are eaten in many parts of India, particularly in the coastal regions such as Bengal. The types of fish caught are different from the ones found in colder European waters, but most types of white fish are suitable for the recipes. In India, fish are frequently cooked with the skin, bones and head intact.

Some of the finest prawns come from Indian waters, so it is not surprising that these are so often used in Indian cuisine. If you are able to buy king prawns for the recipes in this section, you will produce an even finer meal.

1 Fish Curry

Ingredients

45 ml/3 tbsp vegetable oil or ghee
2 onions, chopped
2.5 cm/1 in piece ginger root, crushed
4 cloves garlic, crushed
5 ml/1 tsp garam masala
5 ml/1 tsp ground cumin
5 ml/1 tsp ground coriander
5 ml/1 tsp chilli powder
2.5 ml/½ tsp turmeric
450 g/1 lb haddock or halibut fillets, cut into small pieces
4 tomatoes, skinned and chopped
1 green chilli, seeded and chopped
175 ml/6 fl oz/¾ cup water
Salt
15 ml/1 tbsp chopped fresh coriander

Method

1. Heat the oil or ghee in a heavy-based saucepan and fry the onions until lightly browned.

2. Add the ginger, garlic and spices and cook for 30 seconds. Add the fish and stir gently.

3. Add the tomatoes, chilli and water and season to taste with salt. Bring to the boil, cover and simmer gently for about 15 minutes until the fish is tender. Serve garnished with fresh coriander.

Serves 4

2 Shell Prawn Curry

Ingredients

2 onions, chopped
12 dried red chillies, seeded and chopped
48 large prawns
600 ml/1 pt/2 ½ cups water
5 ml/1 tsp turmeric
Salt
45 ml/3 tbsp coconut oil
15 ml/1 tbsp chopped fresh coriander

Method

1. Grind the onions and chillies together to a thick paste.

2. Remove the heads and tails from the prawns and take out the back thread but leave the shells on.

3. Put the prawns in a saucepan with the water and turmeric and season to taste with salt. Bring to the boil, cover and simmer over a low heat for about 30 minutes until nearly dry.

4. In another saucepan, heat the oil and fry the onion paste for a few minutes until soft. Add the prawn mixture and simmer over a low heat for about 5 minutes until the sauce is thick. Serve garnished with coriander.

Serves 4

3 Prawn Vindaloo

Ingredients

15 ml/1 tbsp Vindaloo Powder (page 13)
2.5 cm/1 in piece ginger root, grated
7 garlic cloves, crushed
750 g/12 oz shelled prawns
45 ml/3 tbsp mustard oil
1 bay leaf
3 cardamoms, peeled and crushed
2 large onions, thinly sliced
1 green chilli, seeded and chopped
250 ml/8 fl oz/1 cup water
Salt
5 ml/1 tsp white wine vinegar
5 ml/1 tsp sugar

Method

1. Mix together the vindaloo powder, ginger and garlic and rub it into the prawns. Cover and leave to one side for at least 30 minutes.

2. Heat the oil and fry the bay leaf for a few seconds. Add the cardamoms and fry for a further few seconds. Add the prawns and marinade and fry for 2 minutes.

3. Add the onions and fry until lightly browned.

4. Add the chilli and water and season to taste with salt. Stir well, bring to the boil and simmer for about 20 minutes until the prawns are tender and the sauce has reduced.

5. Stir in the wine vinegar and sugar, heat through and serve.

Serves 4

Prawn Kashmir

Ingredients

450 g/1 lb shelled prawns
250 ml/8 fl oz/1 cup natural yoghurt
5 ml/1 tsp turmeric
5 ml/1 tsp ground cumin
2.5 ml/½ tsp chilli powder
3 cloves garlic, crushed
45 ml/3 tbsp vegetable oil or ghee
50 g/2 oz/¼ cup flaked almonds
75 g/3 oz/¾ cup sultanas
50 g/2 oz/¼ cup dried apricots, chopped
50 g/2 oz/¼ cup sliced bananas
Juice of 1 lemon
Salt

Method

1. Place the prawns in a bowl. Mix the yoghurt with the spices and garlic and stir it into the prawns. Cover and leave to marinate overnight.

2. Heat the oil or ghee in a heavy-based saucepan and fry the flaked almonds for 2 minutes. Remove from the pan and drain on kitchen paper.

3. Fry the sultanas and apricots until they plump up. Remove from the pan and drain on kitchen paper.

4. Add the prawns and marinade and fry for 5 minutes until browned. Add the almonds, sultanas, apricots and bananas. Bring to the boil, cover and simmer gently for about 20 minutes until the prawns are cooked and the sauce has thickened, stirring occasionally to prevent the sauce sticking to the bottom.

5. Add the lemon juice, season to taste with salt and serve.

Serves 4 to 6

5 Bhuna Prawn

Ingredients

45 ml/3 tbsp natural yoghurt, lightly beaten
1 clove garlic, crushed
1 green chilli, seeded and chopped
2 cloves
5 ml/1 tsp black peppercorns
2.5 cm/1 in piece cinnamon stick
5 ml/1 tsp cumin seeds
Salt
450 g/1 lb shelled prawns
45 ml/3 tbsp vegetable oil
3 onions, sliced

Method

1. Mix together the yoghurt, garlic and chilli.

2. Lightly roast the cloves, peppercorns, cinnamon and cumin in a dry pan until they begin to darken. Grind to a powder and mix into the yoghurt. Season to taste with salt. Add the prawns to the mixture and mix well.

3. Heat the oil in a heavy-based pan and fry the onions until crisp and golden brown. Remove them from the oil and put to one side.

4. Add the prawns and yoghurt mixture to the pan, cover and simmer for about 15 minutes until the juices evaporate and the prawns are tender. Serve sprinkled with the crumbled fried onions.

Serves 4

6 Prawn Patia

The thick, dark brown sauce in this curry is fairly dry. The mixture of tamarind juice, vinegar, sugar and honey produces a sweet and sour flavour.

Ingredients

45 ml/3 tbsp natural yoghurt
1 onion, chopped
2 cloves garlic, crushed
2.5 cm/1 in piece ginger root, peeled and chopped
30 ml/2 tbsp mustard oil
5 ml/1 tsp cumin seeds
2.5 ml/½ tsp mustard seeds
2.5 ml/½ tsp fennel seeds
2.5 ml/½ tsp fenugreek seeds
2.5 ml/½ tsp turmeric
10 ml/2 tsp paprika
5 ml/1 tsp ground coriander
25 g/1 oz tamarind pods, soaked in a cup of water
15 ml/1 tbsp brown sugar
15 ml/1 tbsp honey
15 ml/1 tbsp white wine vinegar
15 ml/1 tbsp tomato purée
450 g/1 lb shelled prawns
Salt

Method

1. Purée the yoghurt, onion, garlic, ginger and 30 ml/ 2 tbsp of water to a smooth paste.

2. Heat the oil in a heavy-based saucepan and add the cumin, mustard, fennel and fenugreek seeds. Fry until they stop cracking, then add the yoghurt mixture and cook gently for 15 minutes. Add the

turmeric, paprika and coriander and cook for 5 minutes.

3. Extract the pulp from the soaked tamarind and push it through a sieve. Discard the seeds and mix the juice with the sugar, honey, wine vinegar and tomato purée. Add to the other ingredients and cook for a further 10 minutes.

4. Add the prawns and season to taste with salt. Simmer for a further 10 minutes until the gravy is dark and thick.

Serves 4

7 Prawn and Mushroom Curry

Ingredients

45 ml/3 tbsp vegetable oil
3 spring onions, cut into rings
2.5 cm/1 in piece ginger root, cut into thin sticks
450 g/1 lb shelled prawns
225 g/8 oz mushrooms, halved
60 ml/4 tbsp natural yoghurt
45 ml/3 tbsp cream, lightly beaten
45 ml/3 tbsp finely chopped fresh coriander
2 green chillies, seeded and chopped
Salt and freshly ground black pepper

Method

1. Heat the oil in a heavy-based saucepan and fry the spring onions until soft but not browned. Add the ginger and fry for 2 minutes. Add the prawns, stir well, cover and simmer for 10 minutes.

2. Add the mushrooms, cover and cook for 10 minutes until the prawns and mushrooms are cooked and the liquid has evaporated.

3. Meanwhile, place the yoghurt in a strainer over a bowl and let the whey drop out of the yoghurt, leaving a soft thick paste. Mix this with the cream, then stir in the coriander and chillies and season generously with salt and pepper.

4. When the prawns and mushrooms are cooked, stir in the cream and heat through without boiling. Serve immediately.

Serves 4

8 Tandoori King Prawn Masala

Ingredients

450 g/1 lb shelled prawns
15 ml/1 tbsp butter or ghee
45 ml/3 tbsp vegetable oil
5 ml/1 tsp mustard seeds
2 large onions, minced
1 clove garlic, crushed
3 tomatoes, skinned and chopped
A pinch of turmeric
10 curry leaves, torn into pieces
Salt
2 green chillies, seeded and chopped
250 ml/8 fl oz/1 cup water

Method

1. Thread the prawns on to skewers and arrange on a rack in a roasting tin so the juices can drain. Bake in a preheated oven at 160°C/325°F/gas mark 3 for 5 minutes. Brush with the butter or ghee and return to the oven for 5 minutes until crisp.

2. Meanwhile, heat the oil in a heavy-based saucepan and fry the mustard seeds until they stop spluttering. Add the onions and fry until golden brown. Add the garlic and stir-fry for 1 minute. Add the tomatoes and fry until the oil rises to the top. Add the turmeric and fry for 30 seconds.

3. Add the remaining ingredients, bring to the boil and simmer for 10 minutes.

4. Drop in the prawns and heat through gently before serving.

Serves 4

9 Prawn Madras

Ingredients

25 g/1 oz tamarind pods
30 ml/2 tbsp vegetable oil or ghee
1 onion, finely chopped
3 cloves garlic, crushed
5 ml/1 tsp chilli powder
5 ml/1 tsp ground coriander
2.5 ml/½ tsp ground cumin
2.5 ml/½ tsp ground mustard seeds
2.5 ml/½ tsp ground fenugreek
A pinch of turmeric
15 ml/1 tbsp desiccated coconut
4 curry leaves
225 g/8 oz can tomatoes
450 g/1 lb shelled prawns
1 green chilli, seeded and finely chopped
Salt

For the garnish:
30 ml/2 tbsp vegetable oil or ghee
1 onion, chopped
5 ml/1 tsp cumin seeds
15 ml/1 tbsp chopped fresh coriander

Method

1. Soak the tamarind pods in hot water for 15 minutes, then drain and extract the pulp.

2. Heat the oil or ghee in a heavy-based saucepan and fry the onion until lightly browned. Add the garlic, chilli powder, coriander, cumin, mustard seeds, fenugreek, turmeric, coconut and curry leaves. Fry gently for 30 seconds. Add the tamarind pulp and tomatoes and simmer for 1 minute.

3. Add the prawns and chilli and season to taste with salt. Cover and simmer gently for 30 minutes.

4. When you are almost ready to serve, heat the oil for the garnish and fry the onion until golden brown. Add the cumin seeds and when they begin to crackle pour the mixture over the prawn curry. Serve sprinkled with fresh coriander.

Serves 4

10 Prawn Pal

Follow the recipe for Chicken Pal on page 68 but substitute 450 g/1 lb shelled prawns for the chicken and reduce the cooking time slightly.

South Indian-Style Prawns

Ingredients

45 ml/3 tbsp vegetable oil
2.5 ml/½ tsp mustard seeds
2.5 ml/½ tsp cumin seeds
2 onions, finely chopped
2.5 cm/1 in piece ginger root, chopped
2 green chillies, seeded and chopped
8 curry leaves, torn into pieces
3 tomatoes, skinned and chopped
A large pinch of turmeric
5 ml/1 tsp ground coriander
450 g/1 lb shelled prawns
Freshly ground black pepper

Method

1. Heat the oil and fry the mustard seeds for a few seconds. Add the cumin and fry until the seeds stop spluttering. Add the onions and fry until just beginning to brown.

2. Add the ginger, chillies and curry leaves and fry for 3 minutes. Add the tomatoes and fry until the oil rises to the top. Add the turmeric and coriander and fry for 1 minute.

3. Add the prawns, mix well, cover and cook over a low heat for about 20 minutes, adding a little more water during cooking if necessary. Season to taste with pepper.

Serves 4

Vegetable Curries

General Notes

Many Indians are vegetarians, so there is a wide variety of vegetable dishes in their cuisine. Vegetable curries are often cooked dry, with the natural juices supplying the moisture and the addition of just a little water to prevent them sticking to the pan. Only small amounts of spice are added so that the flavour of the vegetables is enhanced but not masked. Many dishes include chilli powder, which can vary in strength and should be used sparingly.

Aubergine *(baigan)*, cauliflower *(phool gobhi)*, potato *(aloo)*, spinach *(sag)*, okra *(bhindi)* and peas *(mattar)* are popular vegetables.

Dhals are made from many types of pulses. The most familiar ones are lentils and chick peas.

1 Curry Sauce

You can make up this basic curry and keep it for up to a week in the refrigerator, or freeze it.

Ingredients

60 ml/4 tbsp vegetable oil
3 large onions, grated
5 ml/1 tsp ground ginger
1 clove garlic, crushed
3 large tomatoes, skinned and chopped
5 ml/1 tsp ground coriander
5 ml/1 tsp ground cumin
2.5 ml/½ tsp turmeric
2.5 ml/½ tsp garam masala

Method

1. Heat the oil in a heavy-based saucepan and fry the onion until it is lightly browned, stirring frequently.

2. Add the ginger and garlic and fry until golden brown, stirring continuously and adding a few teaspoons of water if the mixture begins to stick to the bottom of the pan.

3. Add the tomatoes and fry until the oil rises to the top.

4. Add the spices and fry for a further 1 minute. Remove from the heat, cool and store.

5. As a variation, cardamom, cloves, cinnamon stick or any combination of these can be dropped into the hot oil before the onions.

Serves 4

2 Aubergine Curry

Ingredients

120 ml/4 fl oz/½ cup vegetable oil
1 medium aubergine, cut into 6 long pieces
5 ml/1 tsp grated ginger root
2.5 ml/½ tsp turmeric
5 ml/1 tsp ground coriander
2.5 ml/½ tsp ground cumin
120 ml/4 fl oz/½ cup water
2.5 ml/½ tsp salt
2.5 ml/½ tsp sugar

Method

1. Heat 90 ml/6 tbsp of oil in a heavy-based frying pan and fry the aubergine pieces until they are dark brown. Remove from the pan and drain on kitchen paper.

2. Heat the remaining oil in a heavy-based saucepan and fry the ginger, turmeric, coriander and cumin for 2 minutes over a medium heat. Add the water, salt and sugar, bring to the boil and add the aubergine. Cover and simmer for 10 minutes over a medium heat until the aubergine is tender.

Serves 4

3 Gobhi Aloo

This is one of the more common ways of cooking cauliflower in northern India. It is usually cooked in a *kerai*, a semi-spherical aluminium or iron pan which requires less oil than if you use a flat-based frying pan. A frying pan or wok are quite adequate, however.

Ingredients

45 ml/3 tbsp vegetable oil
5 ml/1 tsp cumin seeds
2 onions, finely chopped
2.5 cm/1 in piece ginger root, grated
2 cloves garlic, crushed
1 large tomato, skinned and chopped
1 green chilli, seeded and chopped (optional)
5 ml/1 tsp ground coriander
2.5 ml/½ tsp turmeric
450 g/1 lb cauliflower, cut into florets
3 medium potatoes, cubed
2.5 ml/1 tsp chilli powder
5 ml/1 tsp sugar
Salt and freshly ground black pepper
15 ml/1 tbsp finely chopped fresh coriander

Method

1. Heat the oil and fry the cumin seeds until they stop spluttering without letting them get too dark. Reduce the heat, add the onions and fry until soft.

2. Crush the ginger and garlic together and mix with a little water to a smooth paste. Stir the mixture into the pan and fry for a few minutes until the onions turn golden brown, stirring and adding a few drops of water if necessary to prevent it sticking.

3. Add the tomato, chilli, if using, ground coriander and turmeric and fry until the tomato is cooked and the fat rises to the top.

4. Add the cauliflower, potatoes, chilli powder and sugar and season to taste with salt and pepper. Stir well and cook, uncovered, over a medium heat for about 7 minutes, then cover and cook over a very low heat for about 30 minutes till all the water evaporates, stirring occasionally to prevent it sticking. Serve garnished with fresh coriander.

Serves 4

 Bhindi Bhaji

Ingredients

45 ml/3 tbsp vegetable oil
1 onion, grated
225 g/8 oz okra, trimmed
5 ml/1 tsp grated ginger root
5 ml/1 tsp salt
5 ml/1 tsp ground cumin
2.5 ml/½ tsp turmeric
2.5 ml/½ tsp paprika
30 ml/2 tbsp natural yoghurt
120 ml/4 fl oz/½ cup water

Method

1. Heat the oil in a heavy-based saucepan and fry the onion until golden brown. Add the okra, ginger, salt, cumin, turmeric, paprika and yoghurt, stir well and cook over a medium heat for 5 minutes.

2. Add the water, bring to the boil, cover and simmer gently for 15 minutes. Serve with rice or bread.

Serves 4

5 | Bombay Aloo

This makes a good accompaniment to most meals, or it can be served as a snack in which case you could serve the pieces speared with cocktail sticks.

Ingredients

30 ml/2 tbsp vegetable oil
2 green chillies, seeded and finely chopped
5 ml/1 tsp cumin seeds
5 ml/1 tsp ground coriander
A pinch of turmeric
Salt
2 large tomatoes, skinned and chopped
5 large potatoes, boiled, peeled and cubed
Juice of 1 lime (optional)
30 ml/2 tbsp chopped fresh coriander

Method

1. Heat the oil and fry the chillies lightly until they start to wrinkle and change colour. Add the cumin seeds and fry until they colour slightly. Add the ground coriander, turmeric and salt and fry for 1 minute.

2. Add the tomatoes and fry until the oil rises to the top. Add the potatoes and stir well to coat with the oil and spices. Cover and fry for about 10 minutes, stirring frequently to make sure the potatoes do not stick to the bottom and burn.

3. Stir in the lime juice, if using, and serve garnished with fresh coriander.

Serves 4

6 Sag Aloo

This fairly dry mixture of spinach, potatoes and spices goes well with Rogan Josh (page 86) and paratha or naan bread.

Ingredients

900 g/2 lb spinach
50 g/2 oz/¼ cup ghee
450 g/1 lb potatoes, cubed
2 onions, thinly sliced
1 clove garlic, crushed
5 ml/1 tsp ground coriander
A pinch of paprika
1 cardamom, peeled and crushed
2.5 cm/1 in piece ginger root, cut into strips
2.5 ml/½ tsp salt
150 ml/¼ pt/⅔ cup water

Method

1. Place the spinach in a large saucepan with a little salted water. Bring to the boil and cook for a few minutes until just tender. Drain well and chop finely.

2. Heat the ghee in a heavy-based saucepan and fry the potato, onions, garlic, coriander, paprika, cardamom and ginger until the potato is browned, stirring occasionally to prevent the mixture sticking to the bottom of the pan.

3. Raise the heat to high, add the spinach, salt and water, bring to the boil, cover and simmer gently for about 10 minutes until the potatoes are tender.

Serves 4

7 | Mattar Paneer

Ingredients

1.2 litres/2 pts/5 cups milk
Juice of 1 large lemon
Ghee for deep-frying
30 ml/2 tbsp ghee
2 large onions, chopped
2.5 cm/1 in piece ginger root, chopped
5 ml/1 tsp turmeric
5 ml/1 tsp garam masala
2.5 ml/½ tsp chilli powder
2.5 ml/½ tsp ground coriander
450 g/1 lb fresh or frozen peas

Method

1. Boil up the milk twice on a high heat and squeeze the juice of the lemon into it. The whey will separate from the curd. Separate the curd and tie it in a muslin cloth. Hang it up for a day to allow the water to drain.

2. When dry, place the muslin with the curd under a heavy weight to ensure that all the moisture is squeezed out. This will flatten the curd into a flat round cake when removed from the muslin. Cut the cheese into strips.

3. Heat the ghee and deep-fry the cheese until golden. Remove and put to one side.

4. Heat the 30 ml/2 tbsp of ghee in a heavy-based saucepan and fry the onion and ginger until soft. Add the turmeric, garam masala, chilli powder, coriander and peas and cook for about 10 minutes until the peas are tender and a little sauce remains, adding a little water if necessary.

5.   Add the fried cheese and simmer for 5 minutes.
      Serve hot with chappatis.

Serves 4 to 6

8 Mixed Vegetables

Ingredients

45 ml/3 tbsp vegetable oil
A pinch of cumin seeds
½ cauliflower, cut into small florets
2 medium-sized potatoes, cubed
100 g/4 oz pumpkin, cubed
3 carrots, cubed
2 stems broccoli, cut into small florets
50 g/2 oz fresh or frozen peas
10 ml/2 tsp sugar
5 ml/1 tsp salt
2.5 ml/½ tsp paprika
A pinch of chilli powder
A pinch of turmeric
2 green chillies, seeded and chopped (optional)

Method

1.   Heat the oil and add all the ingredients, stirring
      well. Fry for 5 minutes, stirring frequently, then
      cover and simmer very gently for 15 minutes.

Serves 4

9 | Channa Aloo

Ingredients

450 g/1 lb chick peas, soaked overnight and drained
2.5 ml/½ tsp baking powder
2 cardamoms, peeled and crushed
4 cloves
2.5 cm/1 in piece cinnamon stick
2 bay leaves
Salt
3 large potatoes, scrubbed
30 ml/2 tbsp pomegranate seeds
45 ml/3 tbsp vegetable oil
5 ml/1 tsp cumin seeds
2 green chillies, seeded and chopped
4 large onions, sliced
10 ml/2 tsp ground ginger
1 clove garlic, crushed
A pinch of turmeric
10 ml/2 tsp ground coriander
4 tomatoes, skinned and chopped
2.5 cm/1 in piece ginger root, cut into thin strips
5 ml/1 tsp ground cumin
5 ml/1 tsp sugar
Salt and freshly ground black pepper

Method

1. Put the chick peas in a saucepan with the baking powder, cardamoms, cloves, cinnamon, bay leaves and salt and cover with cold water. Bring to the boil, cover and simmer for about 40 minutes until the chick peas are tender. Drain the chick peas and put to one side. Discard the whole spices and reserve the cooking liquid.

2. Cook the potatoes in boiling salted water until tender then peel and cube them.

3.   Roast the pomegranate seeds in a dry pan until
      they are a dark colour and very aromatic. Grind to
      a thick smooth paste with a little water.

4.   Heat the oil and fry the cumin seeds for about 1
      minute until they darken. Add the chillies and fry
      for 1 minute, then add the onions and fry until
      golden brown. Add the ginger and garlic and fry
      until the fat rises to the top.

5.   Add the turmeric, pomegranate seed paste and
      coriander and fry for a few minutes. Add the
      tomatoes and fry, stirring, until the fat rises to the
      top.

6.   Add the chick peas and potatoes and stir very
      gently to coat them with the spices. Fry lightly,
      taking care that they do not break up.

7.   Add as much of the stock as you need to make a
      thick sauce. Add the ginger strips, cumin and
      sugar and simmer for 10 minutes. Season to taste
      with salt and pepper before serving.

8.   If you cook the chick peas in a pressure cooker,
      add about 600 ml/1 pt/2½ cups of water and cook
      for 12 minutes after the cooker reaches maximum
      pressure.

Serves 6 to 8

10 Mushrooms and Peas

This harmonious combination is often included in party and wedding menus. Though, of course, it can be a lot richer, this recipe is light on spices and fats.

Ingredients

45 ml/3 tbsp vegetable oil
2 cardamoms, peeled and crushed
2 large onions, grated
5 ml/1 tsp ground ginger
1 clove garlic, crushed
2 tomatoes, skinned and chopped
5 ml/1 tsp ground cumin
2.5 ml/½ tsp ground coriander
2.5 ml/½ tsp sugar
A pinch of turmeric
A pinch of chilli powder
Salt
450 g/1 lb fresh or frozen peas
225 g/8 oz mushrooms, sliced or whole
15 ml/1 tbsp cream (optional)

Method

1. Heat the oil in a heavy-based saucepan and fry the cardamoms for 30 seconds. Add the onions and fry until lightly browned.

2. Add the ginger and garlic and fry until golden brown, adding a few teaspoons of water if necessary. Add the tomatoes and fry until the fat rises to the top.

3. Add the cumin, coriander, sugar, turmeric, chilli powder and salt to taste. Fry for 1 minute, stirring continuously.

4. Add the peas, stirring well to coat in the spices, and fry for 2 minutes.

5. Add just enough water almost to cover the peas so that they can cook through and the curry will thicken to the consistency you prefer. Bring to the boil and simmer gently for about 10 minutes.

6. When the peas are almost cooked, add the mushrooms and simmer for about 5 minutes until both vegetables are cooked. Stir in the cream, if using, just before serving.

7. If you use a pressure cooker, add about 120 ml/4 fl oz/½ cup of water and cook for 4 minutes after the cooker has reached maximum pressure. Add the mushrooms after you open the pressure cooker and simmer until they are done.

Serves 4 to 6

11 | Dhal

Made in a pressure cooker, dhal tastes slightly different. This dhal is delicious with plain boiled rice and some sweet and sour pickle.

Ingredients

45 ml/3 tbsp vegetable oil
5 ml/1 tsp cumin seeds
2 small onions, finely chopped
1 green chilli, seeded and finely chopped
2.5 cm/1 in piece ginger root, grated
4 cloves garlic, crushed
5 ml/1 tsp ground fenugreek
2 small tomatoes, skinned and chopped
A pinch of turmeric
Salt
100 g/4 oz/½ cup lentils, washed and soaked in 1.5 litres/2 ½ pts/6 cups water
15 ml/1 tbsp finely chopped fresh coriander

Method

1. Heat the oil in a pressure cooker. Add the cumin seeds and fry until they stop spluttering. Add the onions and fry until lightly browned.

2. Add the chilli, ginger and garlic and fry until golden brown, stirring frequently and adding a few teaspoons of water if necessary.

3. Add the fenugreek and stir, then add the tomatoes and turmeric and season to taste with salt. Fry until the oil rises to the top.

4. Drain the lentils and reserve the water. Add the lentils to the pan and fry until they start sticking to

the bottom. Add the water, close the pressure
cooker and allow it to reach maximum pressure,
then reduce the heat and cook for 8 minutes.
Open the cooker and check that the dhal is tender
and well blended. Adjust the consistency if
necessary by boiling for a little longer or adding a
little hot water. Stir in the fresh coriander.

Serves 4 to 6

12 | Curried Courgettes

Ingredients

60 ml/4 tbsp vegetable oil
A pinch of asafoetida
10 ml/2 tsp cumin seeds
4 tomatoes, skinned and finely chopped
10 ml/2 tsp ground coriander
2.5 ml/½ tsp turmeric
A pinch of chilli powder
3 large courgettes, sliced
120 ml/4 fl oz/½ cup water
A pinch of garam masala

Method

1.   Heat the oil in a heavy-based saucepan, add the
       asafoetida, then the cumin seeds and tomatoes.
       Add the coriander, turmeric and chilli powder and
       fry for 3 minutes.

2.   Add the courgettes and water, bring to the boil,
       cover and simmer for about 15 minutes, stirring
       occasionally.

3.   Remove the lid, sprinkle with garam masala, stir
       again and simmer for a further 3 minutes.

Serves 6

13 Curried Asparagus

Ingredients

450 g/1 lb asparagus
45 ml/3 tbsp vegetable oil
2.5 ml/½ tsp ground fenugreek
A pinch of cumin seeds
A pinch of mustard seeds
A pinch of chilli powder
30 ml/2 tbsp lemon juice
2.5 ml/½ tsp paprika

Method

1. Tie the asparagus into bundles and stand upright in a saucepan with a small amount of boiling water. Cover and steam for about 5 minutes until tender. Drain and cut into 5 cm/2 in pieces.

2. Heat the oil in a heavy-based saucepan and fry the fenugreek for a few seconds, then add the cumin seeds and mustard seeds and fry for a few more seconds. Add the chilli powder and asparagus and fry for 2 minutes, stirring well to coat in the oil and spices.

3. Stir in the lemon juice and paprika and fry for a further 30 seconds before serving.

Serves 4

Rice

General Notes

Long-grain rice is the most widely available and the cheapest, but basmati rice is the best variety to use for Indian savoury dishes. This is also a long-grain rice, but the grains are slender and delicate and it has a distinct aroma and flavour.

Basmati rice grows in the foothills of the Himalayas and it is usually aged for a year before it is sold. This increases the nutty flavour.

Before cooking rice, always wash it in plenty of water. This removes the starchy powder so that the grains remain separate and do not stick together.

Plain Rice

Ingredients

300 g/10 oz/1 ¼ cups basmati rice
30 ml/2 tbsp ghee or butter
600 ml/1 pt/2 ½ cups water
A pinch of salt

Method

1. Wash the rice twice in fresh water then leave to soak in water for 5 minutes. Drain.

2. Warm the ghee or butter in a saucepan, add the rice and fry, stirring frequently, for 5 minutes.

3. Add the water and salt, stir well and bring to the boil. Cover and simmer for about 10 minutes until most of the water has been absorbed.

4. Turn into an ovenproof dish, cover and place in a preheated oven at 180°C/350°F/gas mark 4 for about 5 minutes until the rice is tender and all the water has been absorbed. The timing will vary with different kinds of rice.

Serves 4

2 Saffron Pilau Rice

Ingredients

350 g/12 oz/1 ½ cups basmati rice
100 g/4 oz/½ cup ghee or butter
250 ml/8 fl oz/1 cup natural yoghurt
½ cinnamon stick, broken into pieces
2 cardamoms, opened on one side
6 cloves (optional)
30 ml/2 tbsp sultanas
15 ml/1 tbsp chopped pistachio nuts
15 ml/1 tbsp chopped almonds
15 ml/1 tbsp sugar
10 ml/2 tsp salt
15 ml/1 tbsp cumin seed, roasted and ground
500 ml/18 fl oz/2 ¼ cups water
15 ml/1 tbsp ground saffron

Method

1. Wash and drain the rice and leave it to dry at room temperature. Do this in the morning if you are going to cook in the afternoon.

2. Place the rice, ghee, yoghurt, cardamoms, cinnamon, cloves, sultanas, pistachio nuts, almonds, sugar, salt and cumin in an ovenproof dish and mix together well. Add the water, sprinkle the saffron on the top and stir.

3. Cook the rice in a preheated oven at 200°C/400°F/gas mark 6 for 10 minutes. Lower the heat to 150°C/300°F/gas mark 2 and cook for a further 40 minutes.

4. Check to see whether the rice is tender and the liquid has been absorbed. If not, cook for a further few minutes. Stir well before serving.

Serves 3 to 4

3 | Pea Pilau

Ingredients

350 g/12 oz/1 ½ cups basmati rice
50 g/2 oz/¼ cup ghee or butter
225 g/8 oz/2 cups frozen peas
2 bay leaves
2 cardamoms, peeled and ground
750 ml/1 ¼ pts/3 cups water
15 ml/1 tbsp salt

Method

1. Wash and drain the rice and leave it to dry at room temperature.

2. Heat the ghee or butter in a flameproof casserole and gently fry the rice, peas, bay leaves and cardamom for 5 minutes over a medium heat.

3. Add the water and salt and bring to the boil. Cover and cook in a preheated oven at 150°C/300°F/gas mark 2 for 40 minutes.

4. Stir well and check that the rice is tender and the liquid has been absorbed before serving.

Serves 3 to 4

Rice with Whole Spices

Ingredients

450 g/1 lb/2 cups basmati rice
60 ml/4 tbsp vegetable oil
2 cardamoms, lightly crushed
2.5 cm/1 in piece cinnamon stick
5 cloves
5 ml/1 tsp black peppercorns
5 ml/1 tsp cumin seeds
2 chicken stock cubes (optional)
Salt

Method

1. Wash the rice and soak it in 900 ml/1 ¾ pts/4 cups of water.

2. Heat the oil in a heavy-based saucepan and add the cardamoms, cinnamon, cloves and peppercorns. Cover and leave over a very low heat for 1 minute to let the aromas infuse the oil. Add the cumin seeds and let them darken a little but not turn black.

3. Add the rice with its soaking water. Add the stock cubes, if using, and season to taste with salt. Bring to the boil, cover tightly and cook over a very low heat for 25 minutes.

4. Remove the lid to make sure that the rice is tender and all the water has been absorbed. Fluff up gently with the back of a spoon. Keep the rice covered until you are ready to serve.

Serves 4 to 6

5 Golden Rice

Ingredients

450 g/1 lb/2 cups basmati rice
75 ml/6 tbsp ghee
2 large onions, grated
2 cardamoms, peeled and crushed
3 bay leaves
5 ml/1 tsp cumin seeds
A pinch of turmeric
1.2 litres/2 pts/5 cups boiling water
30 ml/2 tbsp chopped fresh coriander

Method

1.   Wash and drain the rice and leave to soak in water for 30 minutes.

2.   Heat the ghee in a heavy-based saucepan and fry the onions until golden brown, stirring frequently. Add the cardamoms, bay leaves, cumin and turmeric and fry for 1 minute.

3.   Drain the rice and add it to the pot. Fry the rice for about 15 minutes until lightly browned.

4.   Pour in the boiling water, stir, bring to the boil, cover and simmer for about 30 minutes until the rice is tender. Serve garnished with fresh coriander.

Serves 4 to 6

6 Rice with Boiled Eggs

Ingredients

450 g/1 lb/2 cups basmati rice
750 ml/1¼ pts/3 cups water
Salt
60 ml/4 tbsp vegetable oil
2 onions, thinly sliced
6 curry leaves
2.5 ml/½ tsp turmeric
A pinch of chilli powder
8 hard-boiled eggs

Method

1. Wash and drain the rice. Place in a large heavy-based saucepan with the water and salt to taste, bring to the boil, cover and simmer gently for about 15 minutes until the rice is almost tender and the water has evaporated.

2. Heat the oil in a heavy-based saucepan and fry the onions until lightly browned. Add the curry leaves, turmeric and chilli powder and fry for 2 minutes, stirring.

3. Add the eggs and fry, stirring carefully, for about 3 minutes until the eggs turn yellowy-brown.

4. Transfer the rice to the saucepan, add 15 ml/1 tbsp of water and cover tightly. Cook over a very low heat for about 5 minutes to finish cooking.

Serves 4

Biryanis

General Notes

A biryani is a substantial meal of rice layered with meat, fish or vegetables. It is usually served on festive occasions, accompanied perhaps by a yoghurt dish and a salad or chutney.

One particular biryani here, the recipe for lamb biryani, has orange saffron milk poured over the top. This colours some grains yellow while leaving others white. The dish becomes perfumed with saffron as it bakes slowly in the oven.

Biryanis go well served with a green salad, Cucumber Raita (page 142) and a vegetable curry.

1 Prawn Biryani

This biryani is deliciously different. The rice is cooked in delicately-flavoured coconut milk spiced with curry leaves.

Ingredients

450 g/1 lb basmati rice
1 small coconut
750 ml/1 ¼ pts/3 cups hot water
45 ml/3 tbsp vegetable oil
2 onions, thinly sliced
450 g/1 lb shelled prawns
10 curry leaves
2 green chillies, seeded

Method

1. Wash and drain the rice. Soak it in water for at least 30 minutes before cooking.

2. Break the coconut and reserve the liquid. Grate the flesh and put it into a bowl. Pour over the hot water and leave to soak.

3. Heat the oil in a heavy-based saucepan and fry the onions until lightly browned. Add the prawns and stir together.

4. Strain the coconut, reserving the liquid and pressing down to extract as much liquid as possible. Add the reserved coconut liquid and make it up to 1 litre/1 ¾ pts/4 cups with water if necessary. Add the liquid to the pan.

5. Drain and add the rice, curry leaves and chillies. Bring to the boil, cover tightly and cook over a very low heat for about 25 minutes.

6. Check that the rice is tender and all the liquid has been absorbed. Fluff up the rice gently and keep it covered until you are ready to serve.

Serves 6

2 Lamb Biryani

Ingredients

5 onions
4 cloves garlic, chopped
15 ml/1 tbsp grated ginger root
5 ml/1 tsp ground coriander
5 ml/1 tsp ground cumin
A pinch of chilli powder
15 ml/1 tbsp salt
60 ml/4 tbsp lemon juice
250 ml/8 fl oz/1 cup natural yoghurt
750 g/1 ½ lb leg of lamb, boned and cubed
2 litres/3 ½ pts/8 cups water
450 g/1 lb basmati rice
100 g/4 oz/½ cup ghee
15 ml/1 tbsp ground saffron
45 ml/3 tbsp warm milk
6 cardamoms, opened on one side
2 cinnamon sticks, broken into pieces
4 bay leaves
30 ml/2 tbsp chopped almonds

Method

1. Chop 2 of the onions and purée them with the garlic, ginger, coriander, cumin, chilli, 5 ml/1 tsp of salt and the lemon juice.

2. Put the paste in a bowl and mix in the yoghurt and lamb. Cover and refrigerate for at least 2 hours.

3. Place the lamb and marinade in a heavy-based saucepan, add 120 ml/4 fl oz/½ cup of water and bring to the boil. Cover and simmer gently for 30 minutes.

4.   Remove the lid, raise the heat and boil briskly for
about 30 minutes, stirring occasionally, until the
meat is coated with a thick paste. Keep the meat
on one side.

5.   Wash and drain the rice. Bring the remaining water
and salt to the boil, add the rice and boil briskly
for 6 minutes. The rice must not be cooked
through. Drain well.

6.   Slice the remaining onions into thin strips. Heat
the ghee in a frying pan and fry the onions until
brown and crisp. Remove from the pan and drain
on kitchen paper. Reserve the ghee.

7.   Soak the saffron in the warm milk.

8.   Place 45 ml/3 tbsp of water in the bottom of a
large casserole. Add the meat, followed by a layer
of rice and a layer of fried onions. Add a few
cardamoms, a piece of cinnamon, a bay leaf and
some almonds. Continue layering in this way until
you have used up half the onions. Pour the saffron
milk over the casserole then pour over the
reserved ghee. Cover with kitchen foil, then with
the lid to seal as tightly as possible. Cook in a
preheated oven at 150°C/300°F/gas mark 2 for
about 1 hour.

9.   Mix the meat and rice together gently and serve
garnished with fried onions.

Serves 6

3 Chicken Biryani

This dish is best complemented by an Onion Salad (page 42) and a yoghurt. The recipe uses the minimum amount of oil so it is not as heavy as many other recipes.

Ingredients

450 g/1 lb basmati rice
1 small chicken, skinned and cut into serving pieces
2.5 cm/1 in piece cinnamon stick
10 cloves
5 ml/1 tsp black peppercorns
1 litre/1 ¾ pts/4 cups water
45 ml/4 tbsp vegetable oil
4 onions, sliced
15 ml/1 tbsp ground ginger
2 cloves garlic, crushed
1 green chilli, seeded and sliced
2 stock cubes
Salt
30 ml/2 tbsp finely chopped fresh coriander

Method

1. Wash and drain the rice. Soak it in water for at least 30 minutes before cooking.

2. Put the chicken into a large heavy-based saucepan with the cinnamon, cloves, peppercorns and water. Bring to the boil and simmer for about 15 minutes until the chicken is partly cooked. Drain the chicken pieces, strain and reserve the stock.

3. Heat the oil in a heavy-based saucepan and fry the onions until soft and beginning to brown. Add the ginger and garlic and fry until the mixture browns

and begins to stick to the bottom of the pan, stirring constantly and adding a few teaspoons of water if necessary.

4. Add the chicken pieces and chilli and fry until the chicken is lightly browned.

5. Measure the reserved stock and make it up to 1 litre/1¾ pts/4 cups with water if necessary. Add it to the pan with the stock cubes and season to taste with salt. Add the coriander and bring to the boil.

6. Drain and add the rice. Reduce the heat, cover tightly and simmer over a very low heat for 25 minutes.

7. Check that the rice is tender and the liquid has evaporated. Fluff up the rice gently with a fork and keep it covered until you are ready to serve.

8. If you are using a pressure cooker to cook the chicken, turn off the heat as the cooker reaches maximum pressure.

Serves 6

Vegetable Biryani

This recipe can be change subtly by varying the combinations of vegetables. You can used any combination of peas, potatoes, carrots or cauliflower florets. Served with pulses and a salad, it makes a well balanced meal.

Ingredients

450 g/1 lb basmati rice
1 litre/1 ¾ pts/4 cups water
60 ml/4 tbsp vegetable oil
2 cardamons, peeled and crushed
2.5 cm/1 in piece cinnamon stick
5 cloves
5 ml/1 tsp black peppercorns
3 onions, sliced
10 ml/2 tsp ground ginger
350 g/12 oz/1 ½ cups chopped mixed vegetables
2 stock cubes (optional)
Salt

Method

1. Wash and drain the rice. Soak it in the water for at least 30 minutes before cooking.

2. Heat the oil in a heavy-based saucepan and fry the cardamoms, cinnamon, cloves and peppercorns until they stop fizzing. Add the onions and fry until lightly browned. Add the ginger and fry for 3 minutes.

3. Add the vegetables and stir well to coat with the onions and spices.

4. Add the rice with its soaking water, the stock cubes, if using, and salt to taste. Bring to the boil, cover the pan tightly and simmer over a very low heat for about 25 minutes until the rice is cooked and all the liquid has been absorbed. Fluff up the rice gently and keep it covered until you are ready to serve.

Serves 6

Yoghurt

General Notes

It is customary in India to make yoghurt, or *dahi*, every day,
ready to use for different purposes in the kitchen and at
the table. It can be used in a wide variety of dishes and is
also an ingredient for a nourishing and refreshing sherbet
drink, or *lassi*. Mixed with a little honey it makes a tasty
dessert or it goes well with fresh or frozen fruit.

You must buy live yoghurt in order to start making
yoghurt, so check the label before you choose. Once you
have made your own yoghurt, it will form the bacterial
cultures necessary to make about 7 or 8 more batches of
yoghurt. You may then need to buy another pot of yoghurt
to start again. There is no need for special equipment.
Making the yoghurt in a flask maintains the mildly warm
temperature which the yoghurt requires.

Yoghurt

Ingredients

1 litre/1 ¾ pts/4 cups milk
30 ml/2 tbsp natural live yoghurt

Method

1. Boil the milk for 6 minutes then let it cool until it is slightly warm to the touch.

2. Stir in the yoghurt thoroughly.

3. Rinse the inside of a large flask with warm water. Pour the milk into the flask and put on the lid. Leave it overnight.

4. Spoon out the yoghurt into a glass or earthenware casserole. It will keep fresh for a few days if stored on the bottom shelf of the refrigerator.

Makes 1 litre/1 ¾ pts/4 cups

2 Cucumber Raita

Ingredients

2 medium cucumbers, peeled and seeded
5 ml/1 tsp salt
45 ml/3 tbsp natural yoghurt
5 ml/1 tsp cumin seeds, roasted

Method

1. Grate the cucumber flesh and sprinkle on the salt. Leave to drain for 30 minutes and then squeeze out any excess water.

2.   Mix together the yoghurt and cucumber and stir in the roasted cumin seeds.

Serves 4

3 Raita with Radish

Ingredients

100 g/4 oz/1 cup grated radish
Salt
600 ml/1 pt/2 ½ cups natural yoghurt, lightly beaten
1 green chilli, seeded and chopped
5 ml/1 tsp ground cumin
5 ml/1 tsp lemon juice (optional)
Freshly ground black pepper

Method

1.   Sprinkle the radish with salt and leave to drain for 30 minutes. Squeeze out any excess water.

2.   Stir the radish into the yoghurt with the chilli and cumin. Season to taste with lemon juice, salt and pepper.

3.   Chill well before serving.

Serves 4

Spiced Yoghurt

A bowl of spicy chilled yoghurt makes a pleasant accompaniment to a meal. You can vary the quantity of the spices to suit your own taste.

Ingredients

750 ml/1 ¼ pts/3 cups natural yoghurt, lightly beaten
5 ml/1 tsp ground cumin
5 ml/1 tsp chilli powder
2.5 ml/½ tsp sugar
A large pinch of dried mint (optional)
Salt

Method

1. Mix together all the ingredients, seasoning to taste with salt.

2. Chill well before serving.

Serves 4

5 Yoghurt with Banana and Nuts

Ingredients

15 ml/1 tbsp melted ghee or butter
5 ml/1 tsp mustard seeds
15 ml/1 tbsp finely chopped peanuts
5 ml/1 tsp chopped green chilli
2.5 ml/½ tsp cumin seeds
3 firm bananas, thickly sliced
500 ml/18 fl oz/2 ¼ cups natural yoghurt, lightly
    beaten
15 ml/1 tbsp chopped fresh coriander
15 ml/1 tbsp vegetable oil
30 ml/2 tbsp flaked almonds
2.5 ml/½ tsp garam masala

Method

1. Heat the ghee or butter and fry the mustard seeds until they begin to splutter. Add the peanuts and fry for 1 minute, stirring. Add the chillies and cumin seeds and fry for 1 minute.

2. Add the bananas, stir gently and remove from the heat. Stir them into the yoghurt with the coriander.

3. Heat the oil in a small frying pan and fry the almonds until lightly browned. Drain on kitchen paper and stir into the yoghurt.

4. Heat the garam masala for a few seconds in a dry frying pan until lightly browned and sprinkle over the yoghurt before serving.

Serves 4

Yoghurt with Garlic and Cumin

If you only like a mild flavour of garlic, rub a garlic clove around the bowl then discard it.

Ingredients

600 ml/1 pt/2½ cups natural yoghurt, lightly beaten
1-2 cloves garlic, crushed
5 ml/1 tsp cumin seeds, roasted and ground
2.5 ml/½ tsp sugar
2.5 ml/½ tsp chilli powder
Salt and freshly ground black pepper

Method

1. Mix together all the ingredients, seasoning to taste with salt and pepper.

2. Chill well before serving.

3. As a variation, add 5 ml/1 tsp of grated ginger root to the recipe.

Serves 3 to 4

Yoghurt Mint Sauce

Ingredients

60 ml/4 tbsp chopped fresh mint
60 ml/4 tbsp chopped fresh coriander
1 green chilli, seeded and chopped
30 ml/2 tbsp natural yoghurt

1 clove garlic, crushed
5 ml/1 tsp sugar
Salt
5 ml/1 tsp lemon juice (optional)

Method

1. Grind all the ingredients except the lemon juice to a smooth paste. Check the seasoning and add the lemon juice if the mixture is not sour enough.

2. Serve as an accompaniment to most meals. The sauce can also be served as an unusual dip.

Makes 250 ml/8 fl oz/1 cup

8 Lassi

This is a favourite drink in northern India, particularly in the Punjab. Traditionally lassi is made in a *lota* or metal pot and blended by moving a *madani*, a wooden, four-pronged stirrer, between the palms of the hands. This recipe makes a thickish lassi. If you prefer a thinner consistency, simply dilute with a little water or ice.

Ingredients

120 ml/4 fl oz/½ cup natural yoghurt
120 ml/4 fl oz/½ cup water
2.5 ml/½ tsp sugar
Salt and freshly ground black pepper
2 ice cubes

Method

1. Put all the ingredients into a blender or shaker and blend until frothy and well chilled.

Serves 1

Chutneys

*Chutneys are often served to
accompany Indian meals, or with
popadums before the meal begins.*

1 Tomato Chutney

Ingredients

4 tomatoes, skinned and chopped
1 onion, finely sliced
30 ml/2 tbsp mustard oil
10 ml/2 tsp honey
30 ml/2 tbsp lemon juice
1 green chilli, seeded and chopped
30 ml/2 tbsp finely chopped fresh coriander
Freshly ground black pepper

Method

1.   Mix together the tomatoes and onion.

2.   Mix together the remaining ingredients and pour over the salad. Toss lightly together before serving.

Serves 4 to 6

2 Coriander Chutney

Ingredients

2 large sprigs fresh coriander
1 small onion, chopped
1 clove garlic, chopped
15 ml/1 tbsp lemon juice
5 ml/1 tsp honey
1 green chilli, seeded and chopped
45 ml/3 tbsp grated coconut

Method

1.   Blend all the ingredients together to a purée, adding a little water if necessary.

2.   Serve as an accompaniment to a meal.

Serves 4

3 Mango Chutney

Ingredients

30 ml/2 tbsp mustard oil
A pinch of asafoetida
2.5 ml/½ tsp ground ginger
10 ml/2 tsp lemon juice
10 ml/2 tsp white wine vinegar
10 ml/2 tsp honey
2.5 ml/½ tsp garam masala
2.5 ml/½ tsp chilli powder
2 mangoes, peeled and grated

Method

1.   Heat the oil almost to smoking point in a heavy-based saucepan. Add the asafoetida, then stir in all the remaining ingredients and cook, stirring continuously, for about 10 minutes. Serve hot.

Serves 6

Desserts

Indian desserts are invariably milk-based. They are rich and sweet and you need only a small portion. Fruit is often served to finish a meal — fresh mango, pineapple, guava, melon, bananas or whatever is in season. Or you can combine several fruits together in a delicious tropical fruit cocktail.

Kulfi

Traditional kulfi moulds are conical in shape. You can use dariole moulds or ice lolly moulds, although these are a little smaller.

Ingredients

1.5 litres/2 ½ pts/6 cups milk
45 ml/3 tbsp sugar
10 cardamoms, peeled and crushed
50 almonds, blanched and sliced
A few drops of almond essence (optional)

Method

1. Put the milk into a heavy-based saucepan and bring to simmering point, stirring continuously. Simmer until the milk is reduced by a little more than half, stirring occasionally.

2. Add the sugar and stir until dissolved.

3. Remove from the heat and add the cardamoms, cover and leave to infuse.

4. When the milk has cooled, stir in the almonds and almond essence, if using. Pour into small moulds, and freeze for at least 6 hours.

5. Before serving, take out of the freezer and keep at room temperature for at least 10 minutes. Gently squeeze or ease out on to a plate and serve whole or cut into slices.

Serves 6 to 8

2 Gulab Jamun

Ingredients

1 litre/1 ¾ pts/4 ¼ cups milk
100 g/4 oz/1 cup plain flour
2.5 ml/½ tsp baking powder
A pinch of salt
450 g/1 lb sugar
120 ml/4 fl oz/½ cup water
A few drops of vanilla essence
50 g/2 oz/¼ cup ghee

Method

1. Bring the milk to the boil then simmer until it thickens to the consistency of a thick batter, stirring continuously to prevent it burning.

2. Stir in the flour, baking powder and salt and knead to a smooth dough. If the dough is sticky, add a little more flour.

3. Dissolve the sugar in the water and simmer to make a thin syrup, adding the vanilla essence.

4. Heat the ghee. Roll the dough into small balls and fry in the hot ghee for a few minutes until browned on all sides. Drain on kitchen paper.

5. Place the jamuns in the syrup to soak before serving.

Serves 6 to 8

Creamy Mango Mousse

Ingredients

15 ml/1 tbsp custard powder
450 ml/¾ pt/2 cups milk
175 g/6 oz/⅔ cup caster sugar
225 g/8 oz fresh or canned mango pulp
25 g/1 oz gelatine
45 ml/3 tbsp warm water
45 ml/3 tbsp single cream, lightly beaten
150 ml/¼ pt/⅔ cup whipping cream, whipped
(optional)

Method

1. Put the custard powder into a saucepan and blend to a smooth paste with a little of the milk. Add the rest of the milk and stir over a gentle heat until the custard thickens and comes to the boil.

2. Stir in the sugar until it dissolves, cover with a piece of greaseproof paper and leave to cool.

3. Stir in the mango pulp.

4. Dissolve the gelatine in the warm water over a gentle heat and stir into the mango mixture.

5. Stir in the single cream and pour into a mould. Leave in the refrigerator until set.

6. Before serving, turn out the mousse and fill the centre with whipped cream, if using. Return to the fridge until ready to serve.

Serves 4

Tropical Fruit Salad

You can vary the amount of each fruit you use, as well as the fruits themselves. In addition to those listed, you can use apricots, soft pears, papaya or any of your favourites. You can serve the fruit salad with cream or soured cream if you like.

Ingredients

1 mango, peeled and cubed
1 banana, peeled and cubed
A little lemon juice
2 guava, peeled and cubed
1 peach, peeled and cubed
50 g/2 oz seedless grapes
½ honeydew or cantaloupe melon, peeled and cubed
½ pineapple, peeled and cubed
Juice and a little grated rind of 3 limes
Honey
Lime juice cordial (optional)
15 ml/1 tbsp finely chopped fresh mint

Method

1. Prepare all the fruit and place it in a serving bowl. As soon as you peel the banana, toss it in the lemon juice.

2. To make the dressing, mix the lime juice with a little grated lime rind and honey to taste to obtain a pleasant sweet-sour combination. How much you add will depend on the natural sweetness of the fruits you have used as well as on personal preference. Add the honey gradually and keep tasting until you get it right.

3. Add the lime juice cordial if the dressing is too thick. Add the mint. Pour over the fruit and stir gently to coat it well.

Serves 4

Index

Opening doors to the World of books

BOOK TOKEN

Book Tokens

Book Tokens can be bought and exchanged at most bookshops